Southern African

Lbjs

made simple

Doug Newman
Gordon King

*This book is dedicated to Mike King for his depth of knowledge
and training in data methodology techniques, without which
the logic of this book would never have happened.*

AUTHORS' ACKNOWLEDGEMENTS

Special thanks to Pippa Parker, without whose belief in and understanding of our vision this book would not have been possible; also to Leni Martin, Janice Evans, Helen de Villiers, Bev Dodd and Joy Clack for their expertise in design and editing. Thanks to Geoff Lockwood for his invaluable input and advice throughout the project. In addition we thank Sarah Garner, Karen Fick, Joan King and Mike King for believing. We thank the following for their contributions: Patrik Åberg, Tamar Cassidy, Marcell Claassen, Callan Cohen, Jeff da Costa, Eric Ehlers, Neil Gray, Clem Haagner, Ron Jackson, Peter Kaestner, Matthew Kennedy-Smith, Linda Macaulay, Brian McCormick, Mike Nelson, Niall Perrins, Gary Preskil, Peter Ryan, Ian Sinclair, Derek Solomon, Tony Usher, and Tamar Cassidy of the Ditsong National Museum of Natural History.

Published in 2011 by Struik Nature
an imprint of Random House Struik (Pty) Ltd
Company Reg. No. 1966/003153/07
Wembly Square, 1st Floor, Solan Road,
Gardens, Cape Town, 8001 South Africa
PO Box 1144, Cape Town, 8000 South Africa
www.randomstruik.co.za

PUBLISHER: Pippa Parker
MANAGING EDITOR: Helen de Villiers
PROJECT MANAGER: Joy Clack
EDITOR: Leni Martin
DESIGN DIRECTOR: Janice Evans
DESIGNER: Beverley Dodd
PROOFREADER: Tessa Kennedy

Contents

Introduction 4
Birding tips 5
Birding by ear 7
How to use this book 8

Separating families 10
Honeyguides & honeybirds 10
True Warblers & allied species 11
Cisticolas 11
Prinias 12
Larks & sparrowlarks 12
Flycatchers 13
Scrub-robins 13
Chats & wheatears 14
Weavers (females & non-breeding males) 14
Bishops & allied species (females & non-breeding males) 15
Sparrows 15
Pipits & longclaws 16
Canaries & allied species 16

Separating visual groups 18
Honeyguides & honeybirds 18
True Warblers & allied species 22
Cisticolas 34
Prinias & prinia-like warblers 50
Larks & sparrowlarks 55
Flycatchers 75
Scrub-Robins 79
Chats & wheatears 82
Weavers 91
Bishops & allied species 96
Sparrows 109
Pipits & longclaws 113
Canaries & allied species 124

Appendix 132

Illustrated glossary 134

Bibliography 134

Index 135

Introduction

This book is quite unlike a normal field guide in that it has been written specifically to address the difficult problem of identifying LBJs (Little Brown Jobs) in the field. In it we present a methodology that, if followed scrupulously, will guide you to the correct identification of the LBJ in question. The process is cumulative, building on information gleaned at each of three stages: the reader will confront the characteristics first of the LBJ **family**, then of the relevant **visual group** within that family, and finally the **key pointers** that distinguish the **species** which are *only* relevant within that blue visual group. The sum total of family, visual group and species pointers will result in a positive identification at species level.

It is therefore essential to work through the introduction, especially 'How to use this book', and follow each step that will lead you to the correct identification. If you simply flick through the book hoping to find your mystery LBJ, you are unlikely to make a positive identification and will probably become more confused than ever. Gradually, with repeated use of the book's system, you will acquire both confidence and a better knowledge of families and visual groups, and you will have advanced a long way towards conquering the challenges posed by LBJs.

As an example, simply paging through the book to Eastern Long-billed Lark (page 64) will give you the pointers 'long tail', 'habitat' and 'distribution', which in isolation are not helpful to identify the species. If, however, you start at the front of the book and separate first the families (page 12), then the visual groups within the lark family (page 56) and finally arrive at Eastern Long-billed Lark, the cumulative pointers will be:

FAMILY:	robust build
	bill heavier than in pipits
	does not 'wag' tail
	most species ground-based
	forages by walking slowly and deliberately
	usually solitary or in pairs (sparrowlarks in small flocks)

VISUAL GROUP: (BLUE)	long, decurved bill

SPECIES: (ORANGE/RED)	long tail
	habitat
	distribution

This cumulative system gives you 10 pointers for Eastern Long-billed Lark.

It is important to note that, as this book focuses on the identification of LBJs, not all species in a family group are necessarily included. Where species are fairly simple to identify, such as in the flycatchers, they have been omitted from this book.

When you're out in the field trying to identify a bird, observe it closely for some time before drawing any conclusions as to its identity. A quick glance is unlikely to reveal anything about its behaviour and may not even give you enough opportunity to note correctly its physical characteristics and relative size.

Size

Discerning the relative size of a bird is a skill that develops with time and field experience. Remember that when you're using binoculars, a bird at a distance in your field of view often appears larger than one that is close. When you're looking at a bird, it is often helpful to compare its size to that of another species you know well.

Black-eared Sparrowlark
(13 cm)

Southern Grey-headed Sparrow
(15 cm)

Dusky Lark
(20 cm)

Coloration

The colour and markings of birds can vary within a species, so it is advisable to view an illustration of, say, a Tawny-flanked Prinia as a general rather than an absolute representation of that species. The bird you are looking at may, for example, appear to have a larger rufous wing panel than is shown in the corresponding illustration, but this is relevant only if the size of the rufous wing panel (rather than its presence) is listed as an identifying characteristic.

Bear in mind that feathers age, so pale edges can become worn and bold colours will appear bleached. This is particularly important just before birds moult at the end of summer and winter, when plumages are at their oldest and most worn. At these times, the colour pointers that you are looking for may be more difficult to discern.

Tawny-flanked Prinia

Light and weather conditions

Light is crucial when you are attempting to identify a bird as colours often appear different, depending on the prevailing light. This is particularly noticeable for the bill and legs: when a bird is between you and the sun, light can illuminate the blood flow in the legs and bill, making them seem more pink than usual. In cloudy conditions, or if the bird is in the shade, plumage coloration often appears richer than when the bird is in full sun.

Bright, direct sunlight

Deep shade

Photography

Digital cameras have become an invaluable tool in bird ID, enabling you to take a photograph of the mystery bird and identify it later. They do, however, have limitations. Cameras are susceptible to a phenomenon known as 'white balance', which may render the subject more red or blue, making it very difficult to judge the true colour. Furthermore, in both digital and film photography, chromatic aberration, or colour fringing, can add subtle red or blue fringes to the edge of the subject, potentially causing colours to change.

Perhaps the most limiting factor of photography is that it is very difficult to judge a bird's size and jizz from a picture. It is often best to take several photos of the bird from different angles and distances, as well as another species, if possible, to provide a benchmark for size. It is almost impossible to see behaviour from a static image, but you can remind yourself of the bird's habitat by taking photos of the surroundings in which you found it.

Behaviour

As in other animals, a bird's behaviour depends on the situation and will not necessarily reflect the traits you expect when you first see it. This is particularly true of pipits, for example. If you have just flushed a pipit from the grass, it will be difficult to observe its feeding style and characteristic tail-wagging behaviour until it has had a chance to settle down. Thus, it is important to observe quietly and allow the bird to calm down and get used to your presence. It will soon revert to its normal behaviour. Playing recorded calls often alarms a bird, causing it to behave in an unusual manner.

Observe quietly and allow the bird to calm down and get used to your presence.

BIRDING BY EAR

A bird's call is an important element in birding. First, it often serves as a means of locating a bird long before you see it. Secondly – and this is particularly valuable in the case of similar-looking species such as LBJs – the call can be a crucial aid to identification. As you work through the accompanying CD, you will notice how important it is to develop an ear for bird calls.

Don't be disheartened if it takes you a while to get the hang of separating similar-sounding calls. You may think you are unable to bird by ear, but if you can recognise a person's voice without seeing them, you are already able to hear and understand the most important vocal qualities: pitch, tone, inflection and phrasing. The human brain cannot process all the external stimuli it receives, and it develops filters in order to absorb what is important. That is why, for example, in a room full of people all talking at once, if someone says your name you will pick it out. These filters take time to develop and they constantly change as you practise your listening skills. It can take a year or more to be able to hear the subtle differences between warbler calls, for instance. Comparative tracks on the CD will help you get to grips with differences such as these.

Even if you are familiar with the call of a particular species, remember that some species regularly mimic the calls of others. Listen for a while, as a mimic will soon switch to copying another species and thus betray itself as an impostor.

ABOVE: *The call of the Rufous-naped Lark is distinctive and a key 'pointer' in identifying this species in the field.*
LEFT: *In dense bush or forest the call often serves as a means of locating a bird.*

HOW TO USE THIS BOOK

To isolate one species from a large group of similar-looking birds can be a daunting challenge, but it is made easier if the group is made progressively smaller. In this book we have divided LBJs in southern Africa into 13 'family' groups (and allied species); 'families' in this book broadly follow taxonomic groups, with exceptions. For accurate taxonomic groups, see Appendix p. 132. For our purposes, familes have been grouped based on appearance, as follows: honeyguides and honeybirds; true warblers and allied species; cisticolas; prinias; larks and sparrowlarks; flycatchers; scrub-robins; chats and wheatears; weavers; bishops and allied species; sparrows; pipits and longclaws; and canaries and allied species.

Most of these groups have been further divided into groups that have easily seen common characteristics. Each of these so-called 'visual groups' contains up to eight species.

There are **three** basic steps to identifying your mystery LBJ:

STEP ONE: SEPARATING FAMILIES
To decide which family group you are dealing with, refer to pages 10–16 and study the illustrations and family features denoted by pointers and in the accompanying text. Once you have found the family group to which your bird belongs, continue to the relevant page as indicated.

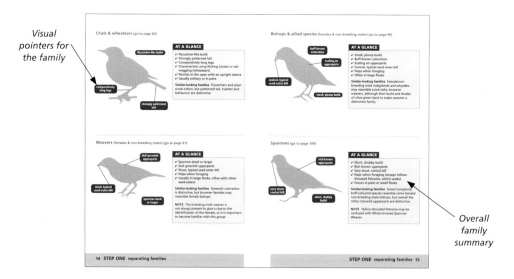

Visual pointers for the family

Overall family summary

STEP TWO: SEPARATING VISUAL GROUPS

Read the general introduction to the family group, paying particular attention to the important features summarised under 'Look for'. Then study the illustrations showing the typical species of each visual group within the family group: the blue pointers show the features that identify each **visual group**. When you have identified the visual group that includes your bird, turn to the page on which the species accounts for that visual group start.

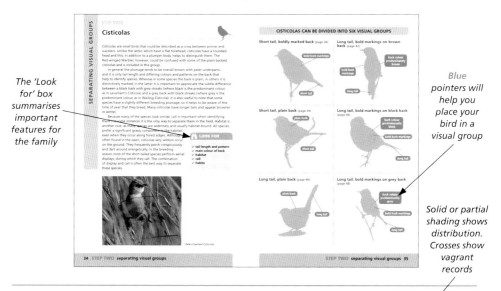

The 'Look for' box summarises important features for the family

Blue pointers will help you place your bird in a visual group

Solid or partial shading shows distribution. Crosses show vagrant records

STEP THREE: IDENTIFYING SPECIES

Check each species in the visual group. Pointers on each illustration show the characteristic features of that particular species, separating it from others *within the same visual group*. The characteristic features are repeated in the 'At a glance' block, which summarises not only the *visual* clues but also other criteria that are important for the species, such as call, distribution and habitat. **A successful identification depends on matching all three features in orange type or one feature in red type.** In instances where a red feature is given in addition to three orange features (for example, '**call**'), it may be regarded as an alternative matching characteristic. Sometimes two red features are given, in which case these too are alternative matching characteristics.

Similar-looking/sounding species as well as CD track numbers and additional notes are given for ease of reference and comparison.

Orange and red diagnostic pointers are applicable for this species only within its blue visual group

CD track number for bird call

'At a glance' delivers all important information in one place

Additional notes to alert you to possible ID pitfalls

STEP ONE

This step depends on careful observation not just of the plumage details of birds, but also of their behaviour and habitat. In some cases it involves listening to their call. Identifying birds, and LBJs in particular, requires patient observation, allowing the bird in question to settle, become accustomed to the birder's presence, and start displaying normal behaviour.

Listed below are the LBJ family groups (as described for our purposes) within the southern African region. Carefully study them and the characteristic features of each to determine the best fit for your bird. It is important to look at all the characteristics in the 'at a glance' box, and to match as many of the characteristics as possible to the bird in question, thereby narrowing any margin for error and pinpointing the appropriate family group.

Once you have chosen the family group, proceed to step 2 (visual groups) and gradually narrow your choice further.

Honeyguides & honeybirds (go to page 18)

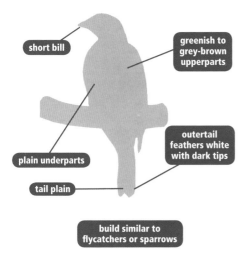

short bill

greenish to grey-brown upperparts

plain underparts

outertail feathers white with dark tips

tail plain

build similar to flycatchers or sparrows

AT A GLANCE

✔ Build similar to flycatchers and sparrows
✔ Upperparts greenish to grey-brown
✔ Underparts plain
✔ Tail plain
✔ Outertail feathers white with dark tips
✔ Bill short
✔ Shy, except when calling or hawking insects
✔ Usually solitary

Similar-looking families Flycatchers; some sparrows

NOTE All these species have zygodactyl feet (two toes pointing forward, two back).

True Warblers & allied species (go to page 22)

Common Whitethroat, Thrush Nightingale, warblers (excluding cisticola-like and prinia-like warblers), rush-, reed-, swamp- and marsh-warblers

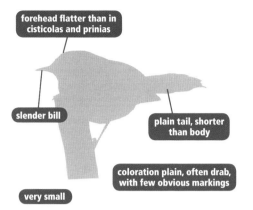

forehead flatter than in cisticolas and prinias

slender bill

plain tail, shorter than body

coloration plain, often drab, with few obvious markings

very small

AT A GLANCE

✔ Very small
✔ Coloration plain, often drab, with few obvious markings
✔ Forehead flatter than in cisticolas and prinias
✔ Slender bill
✔ Plain tail, shorter than body
✔ Occurs in dense cover (trees, bushes and reed beds)
✔ Usually solitary, but territories quite small

Similar-looking families Plain cisticolas; prinias

Cisticolas (Including cisticola-like warblers) (go to page 34)

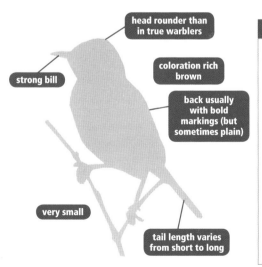

head rounder than in true warblers

strong bill

coloration rich brown

back usually with bold markings (but sometimes plain)

very small

tail length varies from short to long

AT A GLANCE

✔ Very small
✔ Coloration rich brown
✔ Back usually with bold markings (but sometimes plain)
✔ Head rounder than in true warblers
✔ Strong bill
✔ Tail length varies from short to long
✔ Perches prominently or performs aerial displays
✔ Usually solitary or in pairs; family groups when breeding

Similar-looking families Plain cisticolas are like prinias and some warblers

NOTE Lazy Cisticola is the only cisticola that cocks its tail.

Prinias (Including prinia-like warblers) (go to page 50)

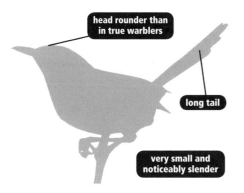

head rounder than in true warblers

long tail

very small and noticeably slender

AT A GLANCE

✔ Very small and noticeably slender
✔ Head rounder than in true warblers
✔ Long tail
✔ Flicks tail persistently
✔ Calls from a prominent perch
✔ Darts very energetically between bushes
✔ Solitary or in pairs or small groups

Similar-looking families Warblers; plain cisticolas

Larks & sparrowlarks (go to page 55)

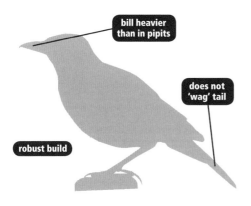

bill heavier than in pipits

does not 'wag' tail

robust build

AT A GLANCE

✔ Robust build
✔ Bill heavier than in pipits
✔ Does not 'wag' tail
✔ Most species ground-based
✔ Forages by walking slowly and deliberately (compare pipits)
✔ Usually solitary or in pairs; sparrowlarks usually in small flocks

Similar-looking families Fine-billed species resemble pipits; conical-billed species are like some female/non-breeding male bishops, indigobirds and whydahs

Flycatchers (go to page 75)

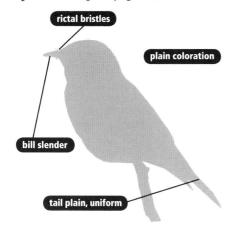

rictal bristles

plain coloration

bill slender

tail plain, uniform

AT A GLANCE

✔ Plain coloration
✔ Tail plain, uniform
✔ Bill slender
✔ Rictal bristles (at base of bill)
✔ Hawks insects – or drops onto them – from a perch
✔ Usually solitary or in pairs

Similar-looking families Some honeybirds; some chats, but habitats and habits differ

NOTE All flycatchers described here have plain tails. Fiscal Flycatcher and Grey Tit-Flycatcher have white on the outertail, but these species are too distinctive to be considered LBJs.

Scrub-Robins (go to page 79)

prominent eyebrow

robin-like build

tail with white tips

AT A GLANCE

✔ Robin-like build
✔ Prominent eyebrow
✔ Tail with white tips
✔ Forages mainly on the ground
✔ Calls very musical, given from a concealed location
✔ Usually solitary or in pairs

Similar-looking families Plain species resemble chats or flycatchers, but the white tail tips are distinctive

Chats & wheatears (go to page 82)

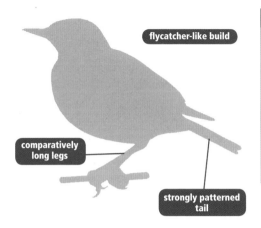

flycatcher-like build

comparatively long legs

strongly patterned tail

AT A GLANCE

✔ Flycatcher-like build
✔ Strongly patterned tail
✔ Comparatively long legs
✔ Characteristic wing flicking (chats) or tail wagging (wheatears)
✔ Perches in the open with an upright stance
✔ Usually solitary or in pairs

Similar-looking families Flycatchers and plain scrub-robins, but patterned tail, habitat and behaviour are distinctive

Weavers (females & non-breeding males) (go to page 91)

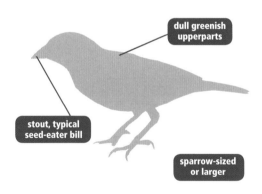

dull greenish upperparts

stout, typical seed-eater bill

sparrow-sized or larger

AT A GLANCE

✔ Sparrow-sized or larger
✔ Dull greenish upperparts
✔ Stout, typical seed-eater bill
✔ Hops when foraging
✔ Usually in large flocks, often with other seed-eaters

Similar-looking families Greenish coloration is distinctive, but browner females may resemble female bishops

NOTE The breeding male weaver is not always present to give a clue to the identification of the female, so it is important to become familiar with this group.

Bishops & allied species (females & non-breeding males) (go to page 96)

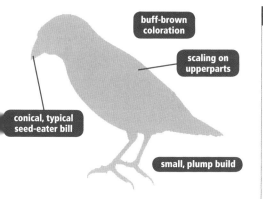

buff-brown coloration

scaling on upperparts

conical, typical seed-eater bill

small, plump build

AT A GLANCE

✔ Small, plump build
✔ Buff-brown coloration
✔ Scaling on upperparts
✔ Conical, typical seed-eater bill
✔ Hops when foraging
✔ Often in large flocks

Similar-looking families Female/non-breeding male indigobirds and whydahs may resemble some larks; browner weavers, although their build and shades of olive-green tend to make weavers a distinctive family

Sparrows (go to page 109)

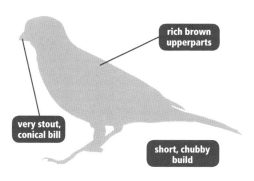

rich brown upperparts

very stout, conical bill

short, chubby build

AT A GLANCE

✔ Short, chubby build
✔ Rich brown upperparts
✔ Very stout, conical bill
✔ Hops when foraging (except Yellow-throated Petronia, which walks)
✔ Occurs in pairs or small flocks

Similar-looking families Some honeybirds; buff-coloured species resemble some female/non-breeding male bishops, but overall the richly coloured upperparts are distinctive

NOTE Yellow-throated Petronia may be confused with White-browed Sparrow-Weaver.

Pipits & longclaws (go to page 113)

bill pointed, more slender than in larks

many species 'wag' tail

AT A GLANCE

✔ Bill pointed, more slender than in larks
✔ Many species 'wag' tail
✔ Most species ground-based
✔ Darts and runs when foraging (compare larks)
✔ Usually solitary or in pairs; sometimes in small flocks

Similar-looking families Some larks, but foraging behaviour and 'tail wagging' are distinctive

Canaries & allied species (go to page 124)

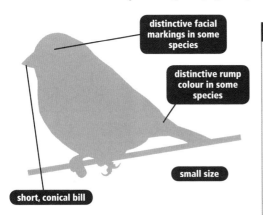

distinctive facial markings in some species

distinctive rump colour in some species

small size

short, conical bill

AT A GLANCE

✔ Small size
✔ Short, conical bill
✔ Distinctive facial markings in some species
✔ Distinctive rump colour in some species
✔ Melodious song
✔ Very seldom ground-based
✔ Often forages on seeding grass stems
✔ Solitary in winter, otherwise in pairs or small flocks; mixes with other seed-eaters

Similar-looking families Plain species may resemble some sparrows; brown species may be similar to small female/non-breeding male bishops; Lark-like Bunting may be confused with some larks

Lesser Swamp-Warbler

Honeyguides & honeybirds

For this family, there is only *one* visual group, so you can proceed directly to step three and work through the species to decide which best matches the bird you have seen.

Honeyguides and honeybirds are reminiscent of flycatchers or sparrows and are also similar in size to, or slightly larger than (particularly in the case of the Greater Honeyguide), the latter. Their plumage is plain – mainly olive, grey or brownish – but all species have white outertail feathers with dark tips. The bills are short, but range from thinnish to stout. The feet are zygodactyl (two toes pointing forward and two back).

Honeyguide calls are usually simple and tend to be repetitive. In some species, individual males call from a specific perch to attract a mate, and will use the same perch over a period of many years.

The birds are mostly sedentary, but show some localised movement in winter. They forage almost exclusively in trees in woodland or forest habitat, where they may be seen hawking insects as flycatchers do (the white outertail feathers will identify them as honeyguides).

All honeyguides and honeybirds are brood parasites, laying their eggs in the nests of woodpeckers, barbets, kingfishers, bee-eaters, starlings, flycatchers and cisticolas. As such, they are usually seen alone, except when pairs come together to mate or parasitise a nest. In the latter case, the male may help to distract the host while the female lays the eggs.

LOOK FOR

✔ upperpart and underpart coloration
✔ chest and/or throat markings
✔ bill size and shape
✔ size

HONEYGUIDES & HONEYBIRDS HAVE ONLY ONE VISUAL GROUP

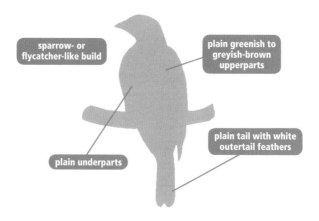

sparrow- or flycatcher-like build

plain greenish to greyish-brown upperparts

plain tail with white outertail feathers

plain underparts

Greater Honeyguide (female)
Indicator indicator
Grootheuningwyser

greyish upperparts

heavy bill

very light underparts

Length 20 cm **Weight** 50 g
Habitat Varied (savanna, woodland, grassland). May be found in well-treed gardens.
Habits Normally located when calling or 'guiding', as it perches in an obvious location to attract attention. Attempts to guide humans to beehives.

 Call Very distinctive *whit-purrrr* repeated many times from a call site. Also an agitated, squeaky, toy-like chirp as an alarm call.

AT A GLANCE
✔ Heavy bill
✔ Greyish upperparts
✔ Very light underparts
✔ Call

 Similar-looking species None

 Similar-sounding species None

NOTE The juvenile is similar to the female, but has a dark cap and yellow underparts.

Brown-backed Honeybird
Prodotiscus regulus
Skerpbekheuningvoël

overall brown to grey

slender bill

belly paler than chest

Length 13 cm **Weight** 14 g
Habitat Open woodland and forest; also savanna.
Habits Usually solitary. Forages in canopy and in grassy areas at edge of forest.

Call Cicada-like rattle repeated three or four times.
Comparative track 152

AT A GLANCE
✔ Slender bill
✔ Overall brown to grey
✔ Belly paler than chest

 Similar-looking species None (the combination of dark coloration and white throat is distinctive)

 Similar-sounding species River Warbler (track 8); White-winged Widowbird (track 119)

Scaly-throated Honeyguide
Indicator variegatus
Gevlekte Heuningwyser

mottled head

greenish back

streaked throat

Length 19 cm **Weight** 48 g
Habitat Coastal, riverine and montane forest, bushveld and miombo woodland.
Habits Solitary or in pairs. Usually located when the male gives his characteristic call from a perch.

TRACK 2 **Call** A shrill, rising screech similar to that of a Barn Owl.

Lesser Honeyguide
Indicator minor
Kleinheuningwyser

plain grey head

greenish back

short malar stripe

Length 15 cm **Weight** 28 g
Habitat Savanna, woodland and forest, including gardens.
Habits Usually solitary. Often located by the male calling from a perch. Does not guide humans or animals to beehives.

TRACK 3 **Call** A very distinctive, double-syllabic *teeu-cheu-cheu-cheu...* (unlike the monosyllabic *tink-tink-tink* of Zitting Cisticola and *tik-tik-tik-tik* of Pallid Honeyguide, which also omits the lead-in *teeu*).
Comparative track 153

Pallid Honeyguide
Indicator meliphilus
Oostelike Heuningwyser

- no malar stripe
- plain greenish-grey head
- very fine streaking on throat and flanks

Length 13 cm **Weight** 20 g
Habitat Forest edges; acacia woodland.
Habits Usually solitary. Unobtrusive; forages in the canopy.

TRACK 4

Call Similar to that of Lesser Honeyguide, but monosyllabic and lacking the lead-in *teeu*; thus *tik-tik-tik-tik*.
Comparative track 153

- ✔ No malar stripe
- ✔ Plain greenish-grey head
- ✔ Very fine streaking on throat and flanks

Similar-looking species Lesser (page 20) and Green-backed (page 21) honeyguides

Similar-sounding species Lesser Honeyguide (track 3); Zitting Cisticola (track 23)

NOTE The greenish wash to the head helps to separate this species from Lesser Honeyguide when the malar stripe of the latter is not visible.

Green-backed Honeybird
Prodotiscus zambesiae
Dunbekheuningvoël

- plain grey head and throat
- greenish back
- no malar stripe

Length 12 cm **Weight** 12 g
Habitat Teak, miombo and mopane woodland.
Habits Usually solitary. Unobtrusive.

Call A series of excited chirps, similar to those of a House Sparrow.

- ✔ Greenish back
- ✔ Plain grey head and throat
- ✔ No malar stripe
- ✔ Call

Similar-looking species Lesser (page 20) and Pallid (page 21) honeyguides

Similar-sounding species House Sparrow (fast chattering; track 124)

NOTE The thinner bill of this species is an additional feature separating it from the similar Lesser and Pallid honeyguides.

True warblers & allied species

Warblers are characterised by having a flattish forehead, unlike the closely related cisticolas and prinias, whose forehead is steeper and head profile is consequently rounded. They constitute a large group of small, drab birds whose coloration varies from rich brown through paler tones to grey and, although some species may have distinctive markings, they are generally difficult to identify on sight alone. Their calls are thus a vital identification tool and it is worthwhile spending time learning them.

Warbling is a descriptive term for rambling birdsong, and it seems apt for the jumbled collection of musical notes that make up warbler calls. The calls may sound quite similar to the beginner, but because of their importance as an aid to identification we regard them as being individually unique (with the exception of those of some reed-warblers) and have therefore not included references to similar-sounding species. Listening to the comparative tracks in these instances will help you to learn the subtle differences between them.

The birds tend to be solitary and are almost always secretive, moving about in reed beds or dense bush without appearing in the open for very long. Although they are often associated with wetlands, many species occur far from this habitat. Most are migratory, spending the summer months in southern Africa. Only a handful of species are found in the region in winter.

Although the Thrush Nightingale is more closely related to the robins, it is included in this group on account of its warbler-like appearance.

LOOK FOR

✔ **call**
✔ **general uppart coloration**
✔ **undertail markings**
✔ **chest markings**
✔ **wing coloration/ markings**
✔ **habitat**

Barratt's Warbler

It is worth noting that African and Eurasian reed-warblers are virtually inseparable in the field on plumage and call, and are best distinguished in the hand, when the comparative lengths of the primaries in the folded wing are helpful. The Marsh Warbler is also very similar to these species, but more experienced birders may be able to identify it by the slope of its forehead. The brief glimpse an average birder gets of one of these warblers as it flits around in dense vegetation is unlikely to be helpful in identification, and it is worth remembering that the Marsh Warbler favours a different habitat from that of the two reed-warblers. While the Eurasian Reed-Warbler shares a similar habitat with the African Reed-Warbler, it is a migrant and for the most part present only in summer (although the occurrence of overwintering birds cannot be ruled out). It is also far less common.

WARBLERS CAN BE DIVIDED INTO FOUR VISUAL GROUPS

Distinctive warblers (page 24)

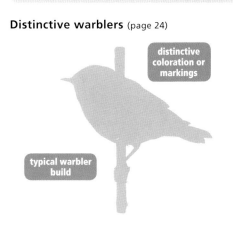

distinctive coloration or markings

typical warbler build

Typical warblers, legs greyish
(page 27)

typical warbler build

no distinctive markings

blue-grey to very dark grey legs

Warblers with barred undertail (page 26)

upperparts brown

typical warbler build

undertail barring or scalloping

Typical warblers, legs not greyish
(page 30)

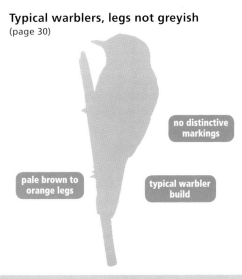

no distinctive markings

pale brown to orange legs

typical warbler build

Sedge Warbler
Acrocephalus schoenobaenus
Europese Vleisanger

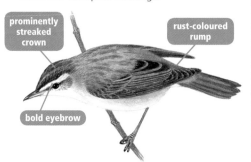

prominently streaked crown

rust-coloured rump

bold eyebrow

Length 13 cm **Weight** 12 g
Habitat Mainly in reed beds and tangled undergrowth under wetland trees. Occasionally in gardens.
Habits Shy and reclusive, quickly disappearing into vegetation when disturbed.

 Call A series of agitated notes. Appears to be trying to copy the repeated phrasing characteristic of reed-warblers but without complete success.
Comparative track 156

TRACK 5

AT A GLANCE

✔ Prominently streaked crown
✔ Bold eyebrow
✔ Rust-coloured rump
✔ Call

 Similar-looking species None

 Similar-sounding species African (track 15) and Eurasian (track 16) reed-warblers

NOTE A summer migrant (October to April).

Thrush Nightingale
Luscinia luscinia
Lysternagtegaal

plain brown upperparts

deep rufous rump and tail

indistinct streaking on chest and flanks

Length 16 cm **Weight** 25 g
Habitat Dense thickets near rivers, particularly in acacia woodland and on drier ground.
Habits Forages in dense vegetation. Although not necessarily shy, prefers to remain hidden.

 Call Very warbler-like, but with a distinctive deep churring element that gives it a robin-like quality. The combination of robin-like notes with clicks and rattles is unique.

TRACK 6

AT A GLANCE

✔ Plain brown upperparts
✔ Deep rufous rump and tail
✔ Indistinct streaking on chest and flanks
✔ Call

 Similar-looking species None (rich coloration of rump and tail is distinctive)

 Similar-sounding species None

NOTE A summer migrant (December to March).

Common Whitethroat
Sylvia communis
Witkeelsanger

grey head

rufous wash to wing

prominent white throat

Length 14 cm **Weight** 15 g
Habitat Dry acacia or broad-leaved woodland.
Habits Skulks in low vegetation, raising crest
when agitated. Flies low and fast between
patches of dense bush.

TRACK 7

Call A rapid jumble of sunbird-like
sounds with no low-pitched notes. Song
often comprises short phrases with gaps
between them, like that of the Greater Double-
collared Sunbird.
Comparative track 154

AT A GLANCE

✔ Grey head
✔ Prominent white throat
✔ Rufous wash to wing
✔ Call

Similar-looking species None (grey
head, white throat and rufous wing
are distinctive)

Similar-sounding species None

NOTE A summer migrant (November to April).

Typical habitats for this visual group

*The Sedge Warbler is a common summer visitor to most
reed beds.*

*Warblers that occupy dense thickets, such as the Thrush
Nightingale, can be rather difficult to locate.*

*Acacia woodland, where the Common Whitethroat
occurs, is not usually associated with warblers.*

River Warbler
Locustella fluviatilis
Sprinkaansanger

Broad-tailed Warbler
Schoenicola brevirostris
Breëstertsanger

streaked throat and chest

undertail barred for at least half its length

Length 13 cm **Weight** 16 g
Habitat Very dense vegetation along streams.
When migrating, also found in isolated thickets.
Habits Very shy and difficult to find. Drops to
the ground when disturbed.

TRACK 8 **Call** A metallic rattle, similar to an insect, or a tambourine being shaken.
Comparative track 152

plain white throat

long, broad tail, barred below for its full length

Length 15 cm **Weight** 15 g
Habitat Tall grass in damp areas and along
drainage lines.
Habits Keeps low in
vegetation, but may
perch in the open early
in the morning.

TRACK 9 **Call** A high-pitched metallic *tseep*, almost like a frog or a ship's sonar.

AT A GLANCE

✔ Streaked throat and chest
✔ Undertail barred for at least half its length
✔ Habitat
✔ Call

 Similar-looking species None (streaked
throat and chest and partially barred
undertail are distinctive)

 Similar-sounding species Brown-
backed Honeybird; White-winged
Widowbird (track 119)

NOTE A rare summer migrant (January to April).

AT A GLANCE

✔ Plain white throat
✔ Long, broad tail, barred below for its full
length
✔ Habitat
✔ Call

 Similar-looking species None (white
throat and fully barred undertail are
distinctive)

 Similar-sounding species None

Lesser Swamp-Warbler
Acrocephalus gracilirostris
Kaapse Rietsanger

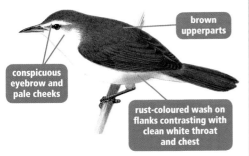

brown upperparts

conspicuous eyebrow and pale cheeks

rust-coloured wash on flanks contrasting with clean white throat and chest

Length 17 cm **Weight** 15 g
Habitat Reed beds in rivers, dams and estuaries.
Habits Skulks low down among reeds when foraging for insects, which it takes near the water surface. May perch at tops of reeds when not feeding.

TRACK 10 **Call** Very full, bubbly and musical, with tuneful notes and yodels. Less harsh and deep than that of Greater Swamp-Warbler.
Comparative track 157

AT A GLANCE

✔ Brown upperparts
✔ Conspicuous eyebrow and pale cheeks
✔ Rust-coloured wash on flanks contrasting with clean white throat and chest
✔ Call

 Similar-looking species None (rust-coloured wash on flanks is distinctive)

 Similar-sounding species Greater Swamp-Warbler (track 14)

NOTE The leg colour is sometimes dark olive-green but never pinkish or light brown.

Basra Reed-Warbler
Acrocephalus griseldis
Basrarietsanger

bold eyebrow

brownish upperparts

no rust-coloured wash on flanks

Length 16 cm **Weight** 18 g
Habitat Reed beds and bushwillow thickets near water.
Habits Less secretive than other reed-warblers. The only reed-warbler that forages in tree canopies.

Call Given in short bursts. Similar to that of the Great Reed-Warbler but less scratchy and less well defined. Reminiscent of starling calls.
Comparative track 155

AT A GLANCE

✔ Brownish upperparts
✔ Bold eyebrow
✔ No rust-coloured wash on flanks
✔ Call

 Similar-looking species Greater Swamp-Warbler (page 29); Great Reed-Warbler (page 31)

 Similar-sounding species Olive-tree Warbler (track 11); Great Reed-Warbler (track 18)

NOTE Best identified by call. A rare vagrant to the region, recorded mainly in January and February.

Olive-tree Warbler
Hippolais olivetorum
Olyfboomsanger

no eye-ring

greyish upperparts

fairly long, heavy bill with orange-yellow bill base

Length 17 cm **Weight** 18 g
Habitat Acacia woodland with tall trees.
Habits Solitary and shy, but responds to spishing.

TRACK 11 **Call** Very full and bold, with a deep, liquid character; includes some grating sounds. Similar to the calls of swamp-warblers, but less musical.
Comparative track 155

Garden Warbler
Sylvia borin
Tuinsanger

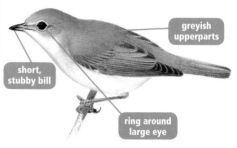

greyish upperparts

short, stubby bill

ring around large eye

Length 14 cm **Weight** 19 g
Habitat Dense vegetation, also in gardens and parks.
Habits Usually solitary, but may occur in small flocks, particularly in trees with soft fruits.

TRACK 12 **Call** Very hurried, the notes flowing together with no gaps between them. Similar to Marsh Warbler call but with regular pauses between phrases and no mimicry.
Comparative track 154

AT A GLANCE
✔ Greyish upperparts
✔ Fairly long, heavy bill with orange-yellow bill base
✔ No eye-ring
✔ Call

Similar-looking species None (size and greyish colour are distinctive)

Similar-sounding species Basra and Great (track 18) reed-warblers

NOTE A summer migrant (November to April).

AT A GLANCE
✔ Greyish upperparts
✔ Short, stubby bill
✔ Ring around large eye
✔ Call

Similar-looking species None (plain coloration and eye-ring around large eye are distinctive)

Similar-sounding species Marsh Warbler (track 17)

NOTE A summer migrant (October to April).

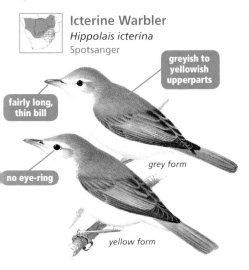

Icterine Warbler
Hippolais icterina
Spotsanger

greyish to yellowish upperparts

fairly long, thin bill

no eye-ring

grey form

yellow form

Length 14.5 cm **Weight** 12 g
Habitat Woodland and riverine bush.
Habits Usually moves around in the canopy. Shy and easily overlooked.

 TRACK 13 **Call** Sustained, purposeful medley of typical warbler notes, including 'kissing' sounds, similar to that of a starling.
Comparative track 154

Yellow form

AT A GLANCE

✔ Greyish to yellowish upperparts
✔ No eye-ring
✔ Fairly long, thin bill
✔ Call

 Similar-looking species Willow Warbler (page 33)

 Similar-sounding species None

NOTE Best identified by call. A summer migrant (November to April). Although no races are recognised, plumage colouring can vary from yellow to greyish.

Greater Swamp-Warbler
Acrocephalus rufescens
Rooibruinrietsanger

no eyebrow

brownish back

contrasting pale throat

Length 18 cm **Weight** 20 g
Habitat Papyrus reed beds.
Habits Climbs up and down reed stems as it forages, and hops from one stem to another.

 TRACK 14 **Call** Full, deep and bubbly. Similar to that of Lesser Swamp-Warbler but more of a chuckle and with more scratchy notes.
Comparative track 157

AT A GLANCE

✔ Brownish back
✔ Contrasting pale throat
✔ No eyebrow
✔ Call

 Similar-looking species Basra (page 27) and Great (page 31) reed-warblers

 Similar-sounding species Lesser Swamp-Warbler (track 10)

NOTE Best identified by call. Confined to a limited range.

African Reed-Warbler
Acrocephalus baeticatus
Kleinrietsanger

Eurasian Reed-Warbler
Acrocephalus scirpaceus
Hermanse Rietsanger

separable only on wing formula

separable only on wing formula

Length 13 cm **Weight** 11 g
Habitat Usually in reed beds and flooded grassland in summer; drier habitats in winter.
Habits Often overlooked; best located when calling.

Length 13 cm **Weight** 11 g
Habitat Usually in reed beds and flooded grassland.
Habits Skulks in vegetation and is easily overlooked. Best located when calling.

 TRACK **15**

Call A series of 2–5 repeated notes followed by a different series; often includes mimicry.
Comparative track 156

 TRACK **16**

Call A series of 2–5 repeated notes followed by a different series; often includes mimicry.
Comparative track 156

AT A GLANCE

 Similar-looking species Eurasian Reed-Warbler (page 30); Marsh Warbler (page 31)

 Similar-sounding species Sedge Warbler (track 5); Eurasian Reed-Warbler (track 16)

NOTE Can only be reliably separated from Eurasian Reed-Warbler in the hand, using the species' differing wing formulas. Inseparable from Eurasian Reed-Warbler on call.

AT A GLANCE

 Similar-looking species African Reed-Warbler (page 30); Marsh Warbler (page 31)

 Similar-sounding species Sedge Warbler (track 5); African Reed-Warbler (track 15)

NOTE Can only be reliably separated from African Reed-Warbler in the hand, using the species' differing wing formulas. Inseparable from African Reed-Warbler on call. A rare summer migrant (November to April).

Marsh Warbler
Acrocephalus palustris
Europese Rietsanger

not visually distinguishable in field

Length 13 cm **Weight** 12 g
Habitat Dense, tangled vegetation in woodland, parks and gardens.
Habits Skulks, often calling from deep within tangled vegetation.

TRACK 17 **Call** Very hurried but with slower sections, as if 'resting'; includes many mimicked sounds, but with no pattern or structure (the similar-sounding Garden Warbler does not mimic).
Comparative track 154

Great Reed-Warbler
Acrocephalus arundinaceus
Grootrietsanger

large size

heavy bill

creamy underparts

Length 19 cm; **Weight** 32 g
Habitat A wide range, from reed beds to acacia woodland; includes maize and other croplands. Often far from water.
Habits Forages low in vegetation, rarely perching in the open.

TRACK 18 **Call** A series of scratchy warbler notes; no other warbler call sounds as harsh. Loud and far-carrying.
Comparative track 155

AT A GLANCE
✔ Call

Similar-looking species African (page 30) and Eurasian (page 30) reed-warblers

Similar-sounding species Garden Warbler (track 12)

NOTE A typical warbler and very similar to African and Eurasian reed-warblers; best identified by call. When not calling, detailed measurements and wing formula from a bird in the hand are the best guide. A summer migrant (November to April).

AT A GLANCE
✔ Creamy underparts
✔ Heavy bill
✔ Large size
✔ Call

Similar-looking species Greater Swamp-Warbler (page 29); Basra Reed-Warbler (page 27)

Similar-sounding species Olive-tree Warbler (track 11); Basra Reed-Warbler

NOTE Although its large size is distinctive, it is still best identified by call. A summer migrant (December to April).

Barratt's Warbler
Bradypterus barratti
Ruigtesanger

Knysna Warbler
Bradypterus sylvaticus
Knysnaruigtesanger

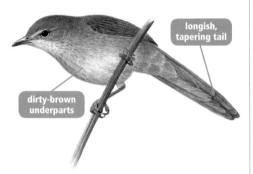

longish, tapering tail

dirty-brown underparts

Shortish, square-ended tail

darkish brown underparts

Length 15 cm **Weight** 15 g
Habitat Dense scrub and other low vegetation along streams and forest edges. May also be found in ouhout thickets along the eastern escarpment.
Habits Remains low in vegetation, often making it necessary to get down on hands and knees to see it.

TRACK 19 **Call** Two or three introductory *cheep* notes followed by a metallic warble. Gets to the warble much more quickly than Knysna Warbler does.
Comparative track 179

Length 15 cm **Weight** 21 g
Habitat Dense, tangled scrub along rivers and forest edges. Absent from forest in which large trees prevent dense undergrowth.
Habits Very secretive and emerges only in response to other species' alarm calls.

TRACK 20 **Call** A series of increasingly fast *cheep* notes followed by a short metallic rattle.
Takes much longer to get going than Barratt's Warbler does.
Comparative track 179

AT A GLANCE

✔ Dirty-brown underparts
✔ Longish, tapering tail
✔ Habitat

 Similar-looking species Knysna Warbler (page 32); Little Rush-Warbler (page 33)

 Similar-sounding species Knysna Warbler (track 20)

NOTE Fairly distinctive in appearance and behaviour, but the call is still the best guide. There is a slight range overlap with Knysna Warbler along the Eastern Cape coast, but the two species can be separated on the shape of the tail.

AT A GLANCE

✔ Darkish brown underparts
✔ Shortish, square-ended tail
✔ Habitat

 Similar-looking species Barratt's Warbler (page 32); Little Rush-Warbler (page 33)

 Similar-sounding species Barratt's Warbler (track 19)

NOTE Although the dark brown coloration is an important feature, the call is still the best guide. There is a slight range overlap with Barratt's Warbler along the Eastern Cape coast, but the two species can be separated on the shape of the tail.

Little Rush-Warbler
Bradypterus baboecala
Kaapse Vleisanger

dirty-looking underparts

heavy tail

Length 17 cm **Weight** 14 g
Habitat Reed beds and flooded tall grassland.
Habits Secretive and difficult to see, but sometimes perches openly, especially in early mornings.

TRACK 21 **Call** A series of chirps with a very distinctive tone, accelerating and sounding like a playing card against the spokes of a bicycle wheel as it accelerates.

AT A GLANCE

✔ Dirty-looking underparts
✔ Heavy tail
✔ Habitat
✔ Call

 Similar-looking species Barratt's (page 32) and Knysna (page 32) warblers

 Similar-sounding species None

NOTE Aside from its distinctive call, this is the only warbler in the group to have an overall grubby appearance and a heavy, often scruffy-looking tail, and to be found in reed beds. Although Knysna and Barratt's warblers also have heavy tails, they are not found in reed beds.

Willow Warbler
Phylloscopus trochilus
Hofsanger

greyish to yellowish upperparts

P. t. yakutensis

very short bill

P. t. acredula

P. t. trochilus

white to pale yellow underparts

Length 11 cm **Weight** 9 g
Habitat Most woodland types, from acacia to broad-leaved; also in parks and gardens.
Habits Usually solitary, but sometimes occurs in flocks of up to 20 birds in a tree. Moves around restlessly.

TRACK 22 **Call** A rapid floaty and descending series of sweet whistles; also a soft, two-noted *too-it*.

AT A GLANCE

✔ White to pale yellow underparts
✔ Greyish to yellowish upperparts
✔ Very short bill
✔ Call

 Similar-looking species Icterine Warbler (page 29)

 Similar-sounding species None

NOTE The shape, yellow wash and pinkish brown legs should identify this species, but the call is also a good guide. A summer migrant (October to April). All subspecies distributed throughout the region.

Cisticolas

Cisticolas are small birds that could be described as a cross between prinias and warblers. Unlike the latter, which have a flat forehead, cisticolas have a rounded head and this, in addition to a plumper body, helps to distinguish them. The Red-winged Warbler, however, could be confused with some of the plain-backed cisticolas and is included in this group.

In general the plumage tends to be overall brown with paler underparts, and it is only tail length and differing colours and patterns on the back that help to identify species. Whereas in some species the back is plain, in others it is distinctively marked; in the latter it is important to appreciate the subtle difference between a black back with grey streaks (where black is the predominant colour, as in Levaillant's Cisticola) and a grey back with black streaks (where grey is the predominant colour, as in Wailing Cisticola). It is also useful to note that some species have a slightly different breeding plumage, so it helps to be aware of the time of year that they breed. Many cisticolas have longer tails and appear browner in winter.

Because many of the species look similar, call is important when identifying them – in some instances it is the only way to separate them in the field. Habitat is another clue, as many species are sedentary and usually habitat-bound. All species prefer a significant grassy component in the habitat, even when they occur along forest edges. Although often found in the open, cisticolas very seldom occur on the ground. They frequently perch conspicuously and dart around energetically. In the breeding season most of the short-tailed species perform aerial displays, during which they call. The combination of display and call is often the best way to separate these species.

LOOK FOR

✔ **tail length and pattern**
✔ **main colour of back**
✔ **habitat**
✔ **call**
✔ **habits**

Pale-crowned Cisticola

CISTICOLAS CAN BE DIVIDED INTO SIX VISUAL GROUPS

Short tail, boldly marked back (page 36)

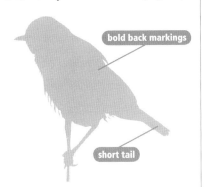

bold back markings

short tail

Long tail, bold markings on brown back (page 42)

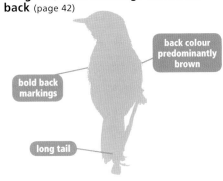

back colour predominantly brown

bold back markings

long tail

Short tail, plain back (page 39)

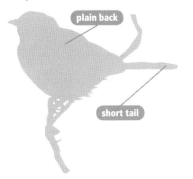

plain back

short tail

Long tail, bold markings on black back (page 46)

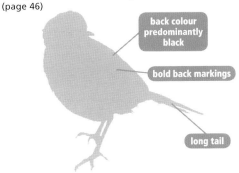

back colour predominantly black

bold back markings

long tail

Long tail, plain back (page 40)

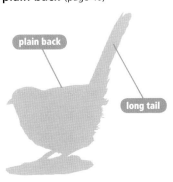

plain back

long tail

Long tail, bold markings on grey back (page 48)

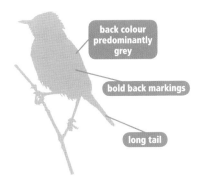

back colour predominantly grey

bold back markings

long tail

Zitting Cisticola
Cisticola juncidis
Landeryklopkloppie

not visually distinguishable in the field – use call

Length 11 cm **Weight** 9 g
Habitat Grasslands, especially where grass is up to waist height. Often around golf courses.
Habits Usually secretive, but perches on grass stems when disturbed. Performs bobbing aerial display in breeding season.

TRACK 23 **Call** A piercing, metallic *tink-tink-tink* repeated during aerial display. Also a fast, agitated 'ticking' alarm call, similar to that of other members of this group.

AT A GLANCE

✔ Call

Similar-looking species Desert (page 36), Cloud (page 37), Wing-snapping (page 37), and Pale-crowned, non-breeding (page 38) cisticolas

Similar-sounding species Lesser (track 3) and Pallid (track 4) honeyguides

NOTE A common and widespread species that is difficult to identify in the field. The call is the best guide.

Desert Cisticola
Cisticola aridulus
Woestynklopkloppie

not visually distinguishable in the field – use call

Length 11 cm **Weight** 9 g
Habitat Dry grassland with scattered trees and bushes.
Habits Solitary or in small groups. Calls from an open perch and during its bouncing aerial display, when it often includes single wing clicks.

TRACK 24 **Call** A series of piercing notes at the same pitch, *tee-tee-tee*.... The pitch may vary from one call to the next, but it remains constant within one phrase. Also staccato notes mixed with wing clicks, like a Neddicky.
Comparative track 158

AT A GLANCE

✔ Call

Similar-looking species Zitting (page 36), Cloud (page 37), Wing-snapping (page 37), and Pale-crowned, non-breeding (page 38) cisticolas

Similar-sounding species Cloud (track 25) and Wing-snapping (track 26) cisticolas; Neddicky (track 30)

NOTE Very difficult to identify in the field; call is the best guide.

Cloud Cisticola
Cisticola textrix
Gevlekte Klopkloppie

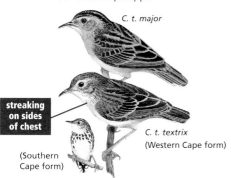

C. t. major

streaking on sides of chest

C. t. textrix
(Western Cape form)

(Southern Cape form)

Length 11 cm **Weight** 9 g
Habitat Short grassland with bare patches.
Habits Secretive, except in the breeding season. Its display flight is level, ending in a dive that is accompanied by rapid clicking.

TRACK 25 **Call** Similar to that of Wing-snapping Cisticola, sometimes with an additional higher note at the end followed by a rapid *chik-chik-chik-chik-chik* that may sound like a wing snap. Also *to-tee-tee-tee-si-si* repeated several times and ending in a rapid *chik-chik-chik-chik-chik*.
Comparative track 158

AT A GLANCE

✔ Streaking on sides of chest
✔ Call

Similar-looking species Zitting (page 36), Desert (page 36), Wing-snapping (page 37), and Pale-crowned, non-breeding (page 38) cisticolas

Similar-sounding species Desert (track 24) and Wing-snapping (track 26) cisticolas; Neddicky (track 30)

NOTE Very difficult to identify in the field; call is best guide. Birds in southern and south-western Cape show streaking across chest. Male has longer legs than other species in group, but as there is little differentiation in leg length among females, this is of interest rather than an identifying feature.

Wing-snapping Cisticola
Cisticola ayresii
Kleinste Klopkloppie

not visually distinguishable in the field – use call

Length 10 cm **Weight** 10 g
Habitat Short grassland, especially where there are bare patches and grass is frequently grazed.
Habits Solitary or in pairs. Secretive, except when performing its undulating display flights in the breeding season.

TRACK 26 **Call** Ringing, high-pitched *I'm-airs-airs-airs* interspersed with wing snaps. The *I'm* is not always audible.
Comparative track 158

AT A GLANCE

✔ Call

Similar-looking species Zitting (page 36), Desert (page 36), Cloud (page 37), and Pale-crowned, non-breeding (page 38) cisticolas

Similar-sounding species Desert (track 24) and Cloud (track 25) cisticolas; Neddicky (track 30)

NOTE Very difficult to identify in the field; the call is the best guide.

Pale-crowned Cisticola
(breeding male)
Cisticola cinnamomeus
Bleekkopklopkloppie

dark lores

plain, pale greyish-brown crown

small bill

Length 11 cm **Weight** 10 g
Habitat Short, moist grassland and grassy pans.
Habits Secretive, except in the breeding season. Perches on grass stem when disturbed. The display flight is undulating, with a repetitive call given at the top of each curve and three cricket-like trills in the dip.

 Call A metallic chatter. Also an almost laughing *tsee-tsee-tsee-tsee* and a trilling, cricket-like *srrrree-ssrrrreee-srreeee*.

AT A GLANCE

✔ Plain, pale greyish-brown crown
✔ Small bill
✔ Dark lores
✔ Call

 Similar-looking species to non-breeding plumage Zitting (page 36), Desert (page 36), Cloud (page 37) and Wing-snapping (page 37) cisticolas

 Similar-sounding species None

NOTE The pale crown is diagnostic in breeding males. With their blackish-streaked crowns, females and non-breeding males are very similar to the other cisticolas indicated; the call is the best guide.

Croaking Cisticola
(breeding female)
Cisticola natalensis
Groottinktinkie

dark subterminal tail band

large, heavy bill

large size

Length 15 cm **Weight** 18 g
Habitat Moist grassland with scattered bushes, especially around pans. Also forest clearings.
Habits Secretive, but perches in the open and gives an alarm call when disturbed. Neighbouring males call from conspicuous perches during the breeding season.

 Call Females and males give similar harsh alarm calls.

AT A GLANCE

✔ Large, heavy bill
✔ Dark subterminal tail band
✔ Large size
✔ Call

 Similar-looking species None (the heavy bill is distinctive)

 Similar-sounding species None

NOTE See also non-breeding male (page 45) and breeding male (page 48). Although the female does not call conspicuously, as the male does, the species' distinctive alarm call, given by male and female, is unique.

Short-winged Cisticola
Cisticola brachypterus
Kortvlerktinktinkie

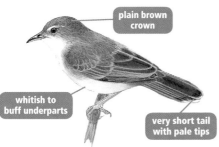

plain brown crown

whitish to buff underparts

very short tail with pale tips

Length 11 cm **Weight** 9 g
Habitat Clearings in and edges of miombo woodland, especially with dead trees.
Habits Usually secretive, but perches in the open when disturbed.

TRACK 29 **Call** A mixture of sunbird-like and other melodic notes, uncharacteristic for a cisticola.

Neddicky
Cisticola fulvicapilla
Neddikkie

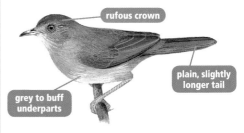

rufous crown

plain, slightly longer tail

grey to buff underparts

Length 10 cm **Weight** 9 g
Habitat Broad-leaved woodland, rocky areas with scrubby growth, and plantations.
Habits Usually solitary or in small flocks. More conspicuous when vocal.

TRACK 30 **Call** Repeated staccato *stuk-stuk-stuk* notes; piercing whistles similar to the call of Red-crested Korhaan, but without clicks; and a series of *si-si-si-si* notes reminiscent of Desert Cisticola.
Comparative track 158

Singing Cisticola
Cisticola cantans
Singende Tinktinkie

- tail shortish and olive-grey
- grey to buff underparts
- small rufous wing panel

Length 13 cm **Weight** 13 g
Habitat Along streams, in bracken and other moist vegetation among trees and bushes.
Habits Secretive; easiest to find during the breeding season.

 TRACK **31** **Call** A series of widely spaced, sparrow-like chirps.
Comparative track 159

Red-winged Warbler
(non-breeding male)
Heliolais erythropterus
Rooivlerksanger

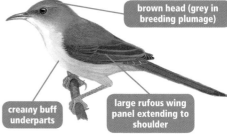

- brown head (grey in breeding plumage)
- creamy buff underparts
- large rufous wing panel extending to shoulder

Length 14 cm **Weight** 12 g
Habitat Miombo woodland with long grass, forest edges and dense riverine bush.
Habits Usually in pairs or small flocks. Moves constantly through vegetation close to the ground, calling to keep in contact with the rest of the group.

 TRACK **32** **Call** A series of excited chirps, similar to those of a petronia, repeated at the same pitch.

AT A GLANCE
✔ Small rufous wing panel
✔ Grey to buff underparts
✔ Tail shortish and olive-grey

 Similar-looking species (to non-breeding plumage) Red-faced Cisticola (page 41)

 Similar-sounding species Rufous-winged (track 36) and Luapula (track 37) cisticolas

AT A GLANCE
✔ Large rufous wing panel extending to shoulder
✔ Brown head (grey in breeding plumage)
✔ Creamy buff underparts
✔ Call

 Similar-looking species None (the bold rufous wing and grey head are distinctive)

 Similar-sounding species None

Lazy Cisticola
Cisticola aberrans
Luitinktinkie

rufous crown

tail very long
and rufous

no rufous
wing panel

Length 14 cm **Weight** 14 g
Habitat Rocky areas with grass and scattered bushes; forest edges.
Habits Clambers about secretively, mouse-like. Cocks tail when calling.

TRACK
33

Call A shrill squeal, like a rubber toy being squeezed, mixed with buzzing and clicking notes.

✔ Rufous crown
✔ Tail very long and rufous
✔ No rufous wing panel
✔ Call

Similar-looking species None (the long tail and rufous crown are distinctive)

Similar-sounding species None

Red-faced Cisticola
Cisticola erythrops
Rooiwangtinktinkie

no rufous
wing panel

creamy buff
underparts

shortish
olive tail

Length 14 cm **Weight** 15 g
Habitat Reed beds and other tall vegetation along streams. Sometimes strays into riverine woodland.
Habits Somewhat secretive, but very vocal in breeding season.

TRACK
34

Call A series of loud, excited whistles, each lower in pitch than the previous one. Also a series of excited trills.

AT A GLANCE

✔ No rufous wing panel
✔ Shortish olive tail
✔ Creamy buff underparts
✔ Call

Similar-looking species Singing Cisticola in non-breeding plumage (page 40)

Similar-sounding species None

Chirping Cisticola
Cisticola pipiens
Piepende Tinktinkie

no visible eyebrow

Length 14 cm **Weight** 16 g
Habitat Flooded grassland pans and reed beds.
Habits Usually shy and quiet out of breeding season, but may sun itself in the open in the early mornings.

TRACK 35 **Call** Two or three *tik* notes followed by a cicada-like buzz. Also some plaintive whistles.
Comparative track 160

Rufous-winged Cisticola
(non-breeding)
Cisticola galactotes
Swartrugtinktinkie

indistinct eyebrow

Length 13 cm **Weight** 13 g
Habitat Reed beds around pans and dams.
Habits Secretive when not breeding, keeping low in vegetation.

TRACK 36 **Call** A series of closely spaced, petronia-like chirps.
Comparative track 159

AT A GLANCE

✔ No visible eyebrow
✔ Distribution
✔ Call

 Similar-looking species Rufous-winged (page 42), Luapula (page 43) and Levaillant's (page 43) cisticolas in non-breeding plumage; Grey-backed (page 44) and Tinkling (page 44) cisticolas

 Similar-sounding species Grey-backed (track 39), Tinkling and Wailing (track 46) cisticolas

NOTE The whistles are similar to those of Gabar Goshawk.

AT A GLANCE

✔ Indistinct eyebrow
✔ Distribution
✔ Call

 Similar-looking species Luapula (page 43) and Levaillant's (page 43) cisticolas in non-breeding plumage; Chirping (page 42), Grey-backed (page 44) and Tinkling (page 44) cisticolas

 Similar-sounding species Singing Cisticola (track 31)

Luapula Cisticola
(non-breeding)
Cisticola luapula
Luapulatinktinkie

indistinct eyebrow

Length 13 cm **Weight** 13 g
Habitat Reed beds and other flooded aquatic vegetation.
Habits Secretive when not breeding.

 TRACK 37 **Call** A series of closely spaced chirps similar to a house sparrow.
Comparative track 159

Levaillant's Cisticola
(non-breeding)
Cisticola tinniens
Vleitinktinkie

fairly distinct eyebrow

Length 14 cm **Weight** 12 g
Habitat Reed beds and tall grass in marshy areas. Sometimes also in tall grassland in montane areas, such as Suikerbosrand.
Habits Very visible and vocal in the breeding season. Quieter and more secretive when not breeding.

 TRACK 38 **Call** A distinctive and bubbly *chip-turalura-lip*. Also a shrill and excited alarm call.

Grey-backed Cisticola
(northern race)
Cisticola subruficapilla
Grysrugtinktinkie

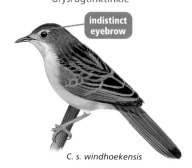

indistinct eyebrow

C. s. windhoekensis

Length 13 cm **Weight** 10 g
Habitat Shrubland and grassy patches on rocky slopes in arid areas.
Habits Frequently perches in the open.

 TRACK 39 **Call** A slow, bubbly rattle, occasionally with a few introductory *chuck* notes. Also a series of piercing whistles.
Comparative track 160

Tinkling Cisticola
Cisticola rufilatus
Rooitinktinkie

conspicuous eyebrow

rufous tail

Length 14 cm **Weight** 14 g
Habitat Dry savanna with scattered trees, and edges of miombo woodland on deep sandy soils.
Habits Very shy, dropping down into vegetation and running like a mouse when disturbed.

Call A thin, metallic rattle with some introductory *chuck* notes. Also a series of piercing whistles.
Comparative track 160

Croaking Cisticola
(non-breeding male)
Cisticola natalensis
Groottinktinkie

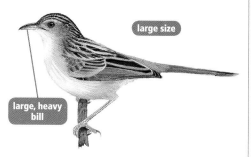

large size

large, heavy bill

Length 15 cm **Weight** 25 g
Habitat Moist grassland with scattered bushes, especially around pans. Also forest clearings.
Habits Secretive, but perches in the open and gives an alarm call when disturbed.

TRACK 40
Call A range of loud, frog-like croaks and buzzes.

AT A GLANCE

✔ Large, heavy bill
✔ Large size
✔ Habitat
✔ Call

Similar-looking species None (heavy bill is distinctive)

Similar-sounding species None

NOTE See also breeding female (page 38) and breeding male (page 48).

Typical habitats for this visual group

It's easy to locate habitat-bound cisticolas, such as the Luapula Cisticola, in reed beds.

Scan the tops of shrubs and bushes to find perching males like the northern race of Grey-backed Cisticola.

The reclusive Tinkling Cisticola can be difficult to locate when it's not calling, even in the relatively open habitat of the dry savanna.

Rufous-winged Cisticola

(breeding) *Cisticola galactotes*
Swartrugtinktinkie

rufous edge
to 2 or 3 rows
of wing coverts

Length 12 cm **Weight** 13 g
Habitat Reed beds around pans and dams.
Habits Secretive when not breeding, keeping low in vegetation.

TRACK
41

Call A series of closely spaced, petronia-like chirps.
Comparative track 159

AT A GLANCE

✔ Rufous edge to 2 or 3 rows of wing coverts
✔ Distribution
✔ Call

Similar-looking species Luapula (page 46) and Levaillant's (page 47) cisticolas in breeding plumage

Similar-sounding species Singing Cisticola (track 31)

Luapula Cisticola (breeding)

Cisticola luapula
Luapulatinktinkie

rufous edge
to 2 or 3 rows
of wing coverts

Length 12 cm **Weight** 13 g
Habitat Reed beds and other flooded aquatic vegetation.
Habits Secretive when not breeding.

TRACK
42

Call *Chip chip chip chip*, similar to the single notes of the House Sparrow.
Comparative track 159

AT A GLANCE

✔ Rufous edge to 2 or 3 rows of wing coverts
✔ Distribution
✔ Call

Similar-looking species Rufous-winged (page 46) and Levaillant's (page 47) cisticolas in breeding plumage

Similar-sounding species House Sparrow (track 124)

Levaillant's Cisticola
(breeding) *Cisticola tinniens*
Vleitinktinkie

olive-brown rump

rufous panel on wing extends up to first row of coverts

Length 13 cm **Weight** 12 g
Habitat Reed beds and tall grass in marshy areas. Sometimes also in tall grassland in montane areas, such as Suikerbosrand.
Habits Very visible and vocal in the breeding season. Quieter and more secretive when not breeding.

TRACK 43

Call A distinctive and bubbly *chip-turalura-lip*. Also a shrill and excited alarm call.

Typical habitats for this visual group

ABOVE AND TOP: Some cisticolas, such as Levaillant's Cisticola, can occur in a wide range of habitats, from reed beds to rank montane grassland. The other members of this group, namely Rufous-winged and Luapula cisticolas, tend to be more habitat bound and are only found in suitable reed bed habitats.

AT A GLANCE

✔ Olive-brown rump
✔ Rufous panel on wing extends up to first row of coverts
✔ Call

 Similar-looking species Rufous-winged (page 46) and Luapula (page 46) cisticolas in breeding plumage

 Similar-sounding species None

Croaking Cisticola
(breeding male)
Cisticola natalensis
Groottinktinkie

large size

large, heavy bill

Length 15 cm **Weight** 25 g
Habitat Moist grassland with scattered bushes, especially around pans. Also forest clearings.
Habits Calls from a prominent perch.

TRACK **44** **Call** A range of loud, frog-like croaks and buzzes.

AT A GLANCE

✔ Large, heavy bill
✔ Large size
✔ Call

 Similar-looking species None (heavy bill is distinctive)

 Similar-sounding species None

NOTE See also breeding female (page 38) and non-breeding male (page 45).

Grey-backed Cisticola
(southern race)
Cisticola subruficapilla
Grysrugtinktinkie

all races except
C. s. windhoekensis

streaked chest or flanks

Length 13 cm **Weight** 10 g
Habitat Fynbos and karoo.
Habits Frequently perches in the open.

 TRACK **45** **Call** A slow, bubbly rattle, occasionally with a few introductory *chuck* notes. Also a series of piercing whistles.
Comparative track 160

AT A GLANCE

✔ Streaked chest or flanks
✔ Habitat

 Similar-looking species None (the streaking on chest or flanks is distinctive)

 Similar-sounding species Chirping (track 35), Tinkling and Wailing (track 46) cisticolas

NOTE The streaking on the chest or flanks varies from bold to quite faint.

Wailing Cisticola
Cisticola lais
Huiltinktinkie

small bill

plain underparts

Length 12 cm **Weight** 15 g
Habitat Montane grassy slopes with scattered bushes and bracken.
Habits Perches in the open, frequently at the top of a prominent bush.

TRACK **46**
Call A buzzy rattle, with one or two introductory *chuck* notes. Also a series of piercing whistles.
Comparative track 160

AT A GLANCE
✔ Small bill
✔ Plain underparts
✔ Habitat

Similar-looking species Grey-backed Cisticola, northern race (page 44)

Similar-sounding species Grey-backed (track 45) and Tinkling cisticolas

NOTE Although the Grey-backed Cisticola is similar, it has 'colder' underparts.

Rattling Cisticola
Cisticola chiniana
Bosveldtinktinkie

smallish bill

plain underparts

Length 15 cm **Weight** 15 g
Habitat Acacia woodland, patches of bush in grassland and sometimes gardens.
Habits Conspicuous for a cisticola and easy to find all year. Calls from the top of bushes and trees.

TRACK **47**
Call Harsh rattling sounds introduced by notes such as *zee-zee-zee*, showing much variation.

AT A GLANCE
✔ Smallish bill
✔ Plain underparts
✔ Habitat
✔ Call

Similar-looking species None (the brown tail is a useful additional feature)

Similar-sounding species None

Prinias & prinia-like warblers

The characteristic feature of all these small, energetic birds is the long tail, which they often raise and sometimes swivel from side to side. Prinias resemble typical warblers in some respects, but their rounder head shape and longer tail give them a distinctive and easily recognised profile. The upperparts are usually plain brown, but the underparts vary from plain to streaked, and some species (Rufous-eared Warbler and breeding Black-chested Prinia) are easily distinguished by their breast band.

Prinia calls are distinctive when compared to those of warblers and cisticolas, but this is not always a reliable feature, particularly in the case of the 'spotted' prinias. These species tend to be bolder and more conspicuous than typical warblers.

> ## 🔭 LOOK FOR
>
> ✔ streaking on chest or throat
> ✔ throat colour
> ✔ eye colour
> ✔ presence of breast band
> ✔ colour of wash on underparts
> ✔ colour of wing panel
> ✔ distribution

Tawny-flanked Prinia

Karoo Prinia

PRINIAS CAN BE DIVIDED INTO TWO VISUAL GROUPS

Plain chest (page 51)

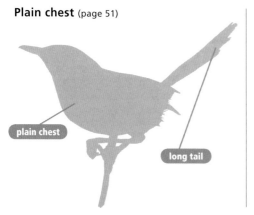

plain chest

long tail

Streaking on chest (page 53)

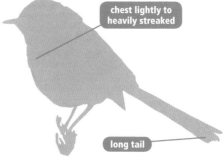

chest lightly to heavily streaked

long tail

SEPARATING VISUAL GROUPS

Tawny-flanked Prinia
Prinia subflava
Bruinsylangstertjie

Black-chested Prinia
(non-breeding) *Prinia flavicans*
Swartbandlangstertjie

rufous wing panel

white throat

buff or no wing panel

pale flanks

Length 12 cm **Weight** 9.5 g
Habitat Grass and bushes along streams and in clearings, avoiding dense forest.
Habits Found mainly in pairs. Forages in grass and bushes, often calling from within a bush.

Length 14 cm **Weight** 9 g
Habitat Dry areas with bushes. Also drainage lines and croplands.
Habits Usually found in pairs. Perches higher on a bush than Tawny-flanked Prinia.

TRACK 48 **Call** A deliberate, piercing *chip chip chip* or a repeated *dzeep-dzeep-dzeep*, less buzzy than the call of Black-chested Prinia.
Comparative track 161

TRACK 49 **Call** A series of *dzzzeeeep* and other notes, more buzzy than the call of Tawny-flanked Prinia.
Comparative track 161

AT A GLANCE

✔ Rufous wing panel

 Similar-looking species Black-chested Prinia in non-breeding plumage (page 51)

Similar-sounding species Black-chested (track 49), Drakensberg and Karoo (track 51) prinias

NOTE Although the rufous wing panel is the most reliable feature, it becomes more difficult to see when the plumage is worn. The buff wash to the flanks, even when faded, together with a lack of a yellow wash to the underparts is helpful.

AT A GLANCE

✔ Buff or no wing panel
✔ Pale flanks
✔ White throat

 Similar-looking species Tawny-flanked Prinia (page 51)

Similar-sounding species Tawny-flanked (track 48), Drakensberg and Karoo (track 51) prinias

NOTE A hint of a breast band from the breeding plumage is sometimes retained in winter. Tawny-flanked Prinia in worn plumage is similar but lacks the yellowish wash to the underparts.

Roberts's Warbler
Oreophilais robertsi
Woudlangstertjie

- pale eye
- grey throat
- no rufous wing panel

Length 14 cm **Weight** 9 g
Habitat Clearings in and edges of dense forest and bush.
Habits Found in pairs or small groups, sometimes in mixed bird parties.

TRACK 50 **Call** Reminiscent of the call of Green Wood-Hoopoe, but faster and higher pitched, like an excited laugh.

AT A GLANCE

- ✔ No rufous wing panel
- ✔ Pale eye
- ✔ Grey throat
- ✔ Call

Similar-looking species None

Similar-sounding species None

Typical habitats for this visual group

Grassy and bushy riverine habitats are an ideal place to find the Tawny-flanked Prinia.

The Black-chested Prinia prefers drier areas with bushes, upon which it perches while calling.

Dense habitat is the favoured home of Roberts's Warbler.

Drakensberg Prinia
Prinia hypoxantha
Drakensberglangstertjie

pale eye

no streaking
on throat

light streaking
on chest

Length 14 cm **Weight** 10 g
Habitat Grass and bushes along rivers, on hillsides and at forest edges.
Habits Found in pairs or small groups. Moves from high altitude to lower areas in winter.

Call Very similar *dzzzeeeep* to other prinias, but with an excited introductory *pree-pree-pree*. Very difficult to separate from Karoo Prinia on call alone.
Comparative track 161

AT A GLANCE
✔ No streaking on throat
✔ Light streaking on chest
✔ Pale eye

Similar-looking species Karoo Prinia (page 53)

Similar-sounding species Tawny-flanked (track 48), Black-chested (track 49) and Karoo (track 51) prinias

NOTE Juvenile Karoo Prinia looks very similar, but the underparts are more sulphur yellow and the throat is streaked.

Karoo Prinia
Prinia maculosa
Karoolangstertjie

dark eye

adult

juvenile

streaking
on throat

heavy streaking
on underparts

Length 14 cm **Weight** 10 g
Habitat Varied shrublands and fynbos.
Habits Found in pairs or small groups. Calls from a prominent perch, diving into the undergrowth if it feels threatened.

TRACK
51

Call Very similar *dzzzeeeep* to other prinias, but with an introductory excited *pree-pree-pree*. Very difficult to separate from Drakensberg Prinia on call alone.
Comparative track 161

AT A GLANCE
✔ Streaking on throat
✔ Heavy streaking on underparts
✔ Dark eye

Similar-looking species Drakensberg Prinia (page 53)

Similar-sounding species Tawny-flanked (track 48), Black-chested (track 49) and Drakensberg prinias

NOTE Drakensberg Prinia looks very similar to juvenile Karoo Prinia, but the underparts are less sulphur-yellow and the throat is not streaked.

Namaqua Warbler
Phragmacia substriata
Namakwalangstertjie

dark eye

light streaking on chest

Length 14 cm **Weight** 12 g
Habitat Thick bush and reed beds near streams.
Habits Found singly or in pairs or small groups.
Seldom emerges from the dense bush in which it
forages, although sometimes feeds on the ground.

TRACK 52 **Call** A distinctive metallic *chi-chi-chi-chrrrrrrr*, reminiscent of the call of Little Swift.

AT A GLANCE

✔ Light streaking on chest
✔ Dark eye
✔ Distribution
✔ Call

 Similar-looking species None
(combination of dark eye and light
streaking is distinctive)

 Similar-sounding species None

NOTE Its range does not overlap with that of
the similar Drakensberg Prinia.

Typical habitats for this visual group

*In the drier Karoo habitats, the Namaqua Warbler tends
to favour thick bush and reed beds near streams.*

*The Karoo Prinia is the most likely prinia to be found
in shrublands and fynbos.*

*Montane grassland and bushy areas along the
escarpment are good places to spot the
Drakensberg Prinia.*

Larks & sparrowlarks

Larks are, in general, ground-dwelling birds and, as a group, are sometimes confused with pipits, which are also terrestrial. However, a foraging lark moves slowly and pecks at the ground as it looks for seeds, whereas a pipit darts and runs as it hunts insects. Larks are also more robustly built than pipits and generally don't 'stand as tall'.

Lark plumage tends to be well marked and richly coloured, with a brown that is 'warmer' than a pipit's coloration. Variation in the colours of lark species depends to a certain extent on the soil colour of its habitat. There is variation, too, in bill shape, from small and conical to long and decurved, but lark bills are always more robust than the thin bills of pipits.

Bill shape is a defining feature when assigning larks to a visual group. Conical bills can be either small or stout, but they will always be short and symmetrical, with barely any curve. Long and decurved bills tend to look thinner, but that is only because of their length in relation to their width. Even the shortest bill in this group, belonging to the Spike-heeled Lark, is clearly long and curves down towards the tip. A third, or intermediate, group comprises larks with bills that are neither conical nor long and decurved. It includes the Rufous-naped Lark, for example, whose bill is shaped like that of the Karoo Thrush.

Belly colour is also an important determinant when assigning larks to a group and it helps to be able to recognise the base colour; even if there are streaks or spots on the belly, you will see that the background is either white or buffy. It is fairly easy to separate larks into six groups based on bill shape and belly colour.

When comparing the size of lark species, be aware that males and females can differ in weight by as much as 20 per cent and that this will be reflected in their build.

The calls of larks are reasonably distinctive and play a valuable role in species identification.

Short-clawed Lark

LOOK FOR

- ✔ bill shape
- ✔ belly colour
- ✔ markings on chest and/or belly
- ✔ colour of bare parts
- ✔ coloration of and markings on wing
- ✔ distribution
- ✔ habitat
- ✔ call

Conical bill, white belly (page 57)

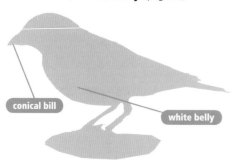

conical bill

white belly

Intermediate bill shape, white belly (page 66)

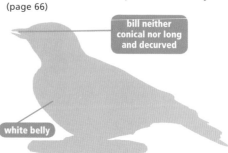

bill neither conical nor long and decurved

white belly

Conical bill, belly not white (page 60)

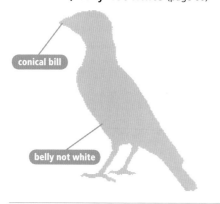

conical bill

belly not white

Intermediate bill shape, belly not white, back scaled (page 70)

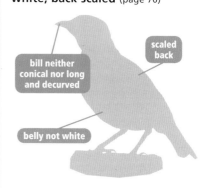

scaled back

bill neither conical nor long and decurved

belly not white

Long, decurved bill (page 62)

long, decurved bill

Intermediate bill shape, belly not white, back streaked or mottled (page 72)

back streaked or mottled

bill neither conical nor long and decurved

belly not white

Typical habitats for this visual group

TOP AND ABOVE: Sparse grassland on stony soils and arid Karoo scrubland make ideal habitats for all but Rudd's and Botha's larks within this group.

Scan heavily grazed areas, which can reveal feeding Rudd's or Botha's larks.

Black-eared Sparrowlark
(female) *Eremopterix australis*
Swartoorlewerik

strongly marked back

heavily streaked underparts

grey legs

Length 13 cm **Weight** 14 g
Habitat Arid karoo shrubland on red soils, and stony ground.
Habits In groups of up to 50 birds. Easily flushed and flies far when disturbed.

TRACK **53**

Call Similar to that of Little Bee-eater. Also chirps like those of Sclater's Lark but sparrow-like rather than reminiscent of European Bee-eater. Other, less dominant chirps are like those of House Sparrow. **Comparative track** 164

AT A GLANCE

✔ Heavily streaked underparts
✔ Strongly marked back
✔ Grey legs

 Similar-looking species None (the heavy streaking and grey legs are distinctive)

 Similar-sounding species Sclater's Lark (track 80)

NOTE No belly patch (compare female Chestnut-backed and Grey-backed sparrowlarks, page 60).

Stark's Lark
Spizocorys starki
Woestynlewerik

pale form   dark form   **pale eye-ring**

greyish bill

plumage colour variable

buffy, faintly streaked breast band

Length 13 cm **Weight** 19 g
Habitat Flat arid and semi-arid land with sparse grass cover, often where the ground is stony.
Habits When not breeding, sometimes occurs in very large flocks on new-growth green grass.

Call An over-excited version of the Cape Sparrow's morning call, with closely packed, sparrow-like chirps repeated in groups of two to five similar-sounding notes.

AT A GLANCE

✔ Greyish bill
✔ Pale eye-ring
✔ Buffy, faintly streaked breast band
✔ Call

Similar-looking species None (the bill colour and breast band are distinctive)

Similar-sounding species None

NOTE Long feathers on the crown form a crest, which can be raised.

Gray's Lark
Ammomanopsis grayi
Namiblewerik

very plain upperparts

A. g. grayi

A. g. hoeschi

white from throat to vent

grey legs

Length 14 cm **Weight** 21 g
Habitat Gravel soils with grasses and shrubs; absent from sand dunes and desert.
Habits Often in small groups. Does not flush easily.

TRACK 54

Call A sequence of chirps similar to that of Pin-tailed Whydah, as well as a lower *foo-foo-foo*. Also a rising *soo-eeee* like Black-throated Canary, mixed with soft, high-pitched chirps.
Comparative track 163

AT A GLANCE

✔ Very plain upperparts
✔ White from throat to vent
✔ Grey legs

Similar-looking species None (the very plain upperparts are distinctive)

Similar-sounding species Pin-tailed Whydah (track 107); Black-throated Canary (track 143)

Rudd's Lark
Heteromirafra ruddi
Drakensberglewerik

dark cap with pale central stripe

Length 14 cm **Weight** 26 g
Habitat Upland grassland, usually on hill-tops with short grass that is regularly burned.
Habits Easily overlooked unless singing. Has an upright stance.

 TRACK 55 **Call** A very nasal, buzzy *tzi-ri-ri-oo*. The rhythm and tone are quite distinctive.

AT A GLANCE

✔ Dark cap with pale central stripe
✔ Call

 Similar-looking species None (the crown stripe is distinctive)

 Similar-sounding species None

NOTE The crown stripe starts at the base of the bill and in some cases may extend only halfway to the back of the head.

Botha's Lark
Spizocorys fringillaris
Vaalrivierlewerik

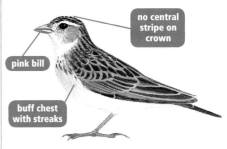

no central stripe on crown

pink bill

buff chest with streaks

Length 14 cm **Weight** 18 g
Habitat Heavily grazed short grass in upland grassland.
Habits In pairs or small groups. Well camouflaged, but white outertail feathers obvious when the tail fans out on take-off.

TRACK 56 **Call** A buzzy, double-noted trill-whistle *chi-ree*, the first note being much shorter than the second, with barely a gap separating them. This is very rarely accompanied by any other sound. **Comparative track** 162

AT A GLANCE

✔ Pink bill
✔ Buff chest with streaks
✔ No central stripe on crown

 Similar-looking species None (the pink bill and lack of crown stripe are distinctive)

 Similar-sounding species Pink-billed (track 59) and Red-capped (track 73) larks

NOTE Some birds may have a slightly buff wash on the belly.

Chestnut-backed Sparrowlark (female)
Eremopterix leucotis
Rooiruglewerik

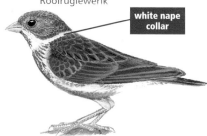

white nape collar

Length 13 cm **Weight** 22 g
Habitat Arid woodland and grassland, favouring burned areas and croplands; also sports fields.
Habits Usually in small groups, but also seen in large flocks. Circles an area when flushed.

TRACK 57 Call A distinct high-pitched *pree-ree*. Also a continuous, weaver-like 'swizzling' interspersed with sparrow-like chirps.
Comparative track 162

AT A GLANCE

✔ White nape collar
✔ Call

 Similar-looking species None (the white nape collar is distinctive)

 Similar-sounding species None

NOTE A dark belly patch places the female of this species in this group. In some individuals the collar does not extend all the way round the back of the neck.

Grey-backed Sparrowlark
(female) *Eremopterix verticalis*
Grysruglewerik

no nape collar

greyish back

pale greyish bill

Length 13 cm **Weight** 17 g
Habitat Arid grassland and karoo, favouring flat areas.
Habits Usually in small groups, but sometimes seen in large flocks at waterholes.

TRACK 58 Call Jumbled notes like those of white-eyes, each phrase ending with a distinctive, rising *pree-ree-oo*. Sometimes sounds quite agitated.

AT A GLANCE

✔ No nape collar
✔ Pale greyish bill
✔ Greyish back
✔ Call

 Similar-looking species None (the combination of grey legs and grey back is distinctive)

 Similar-sounding species None

NOTE A dark belly patch places the female of this species in this group.

Pink-billed Lark
Spizocorys conirostris
Pienkbeklewerik

no nape collar

brownish back (paler in western races)

pink bill

Length 13 cm **Weight** 14 g
Habitat Ranges from burned grassland and freshly ploughed croplands to sports fields.
Habits Easily overlooked. Rarely perches in the open and runs across open ground from one patch of grass to another.

TRACK 59

Call A double-noted trill, with both notes of equal length and a short but noticeable gap between them. Sometimes the call comprises three-noted trills interspersed with jumbled musical phrases.

Comparative track 162

AT A GLANCE

✔ No nape collar
✔ Pink bill
✔ Brownish back (paler in western races)

 Similar-looking species None (the pink bill is distinctive)

 Similar-sounding species Botha's (track 56) and Red-capped (track 73) larks

NOTE The range of the pale-bellied race does not overlap with that of the similar Botha's Lark.

Typical habitats for this visual group

All the species in this group can be found on burned land, sports fields and ploughed croplands, although the Grey-backed Sparrowlark is unlikely to be found on sports fields.

Cape Long-billed Lark
Certhilauda curvirostris
Weskuslangbeklewerik

Agulhas Long-billed Lark
Certhilauda brevirostris
Overberglangbeklewerik

Length 22 cm **Weight** 60 g
Habitat Coastal scrub and old farmlands with patchy vegetation.
Habits Forages mainly alone or in pairs.

 TRACK 60 **Call** A piercing descending whistle given either when perched or in display flight.
Comparative track 165

Length 19 cm **Weight** 45 g
Habitat Short grassland and old farmland with short grass, mainly on stony ground.
Habits Forages mainly alone or in pairs.

 TRACK 61 **Call** A piercing whistle rising and falling in two parts, given either when perched or in display flight.
Comparative track 165

AT A GLANCE
✔ Long tail
✔ Habitat
✔ Distribution

 Similar-looking species Agulhas (page 62), Karoo (page 63), Benguela (page 63) and Eastern (page 64) long-billed larks; Short-clawed Lark (page 64)

 Similar-sounding species Agulhas (track 61), Karoo (track 62), Benguela (track 63) and Eastern (track 64) long-billed larks; Short-clawed Lark (track 65)

NOTE Distribution is crucial for identification as plumage coloration depends on the colour of the local soil.

AT A GLANCE
✔ Long tail
✔ Habitat
✔ Distribution

 Similar-looking species Cape (page 62), Karoo (page 63), Benguela (page 63) and Eastern (page 64) long-billed larks; Short-clawed Lark (page 64)

 Similar-sounding species Cape (track 60), Karoo (track 62), Benguela (track 63) and Eastern (track 64) long-billed larks; Short-clawed Lark (track 65)

NOTE Distribution is crucial for identification as plumage coloration depends on the colour of the local soil.

Karoo Long-billed Lark
Certhilauda subcoronata
Karoolangbeklewerik

Benguela Long-billed Lark
Certhilauda benguelensis
Kaokolangbeklewerik

long tail

long tail

Length 20 cm **Weight** 40 g
Habitat Karoo scrub on stony ground, particularly on reddish soils.
Habits Forages mainly alone or in pairs.

 Call A piercing descending whistle, given either when perched or in display flight.
Comparative track 165

Length 19 cm **Weight** 50 g
Habitat Arid scrub on stony ground.
Habits Forages mainly alone or in pairs.

 Call A piercing descending whistle, given either when perched or in display flight.
Comparative track 165

AT A GLANCE

✔ Long tail
✔ Habitat
✔ Distribution

 Similar-looking species Cape (page 62), Agulhas (page 62), Benguela (page 63) and Eastern (page 64) long-billed larks; Short-clawed Lark (page 64)

 Similar-sounding species Cape (track 60), Agulhas (track 61), Benguela (track 63) and Eastern (track 64) long-billed larks; Short-clawed Lark (track 65)

NOTE Distribution is crucial for identification as plumage coloration depends on the colour of the local soil.

AT A GLANCE

✔ Long tail
✔ Habitat
✔ Distribution

 Similar-looking species Cape (page 62), Agulhas (page 62), Karoo (page 63) and Eastern (page 64) long-billed larks; Short-clawed Lark (page 64)

 Similar-sounding species Cape (track 60), Agulhas (track 61), Karoo (track 62) and Eastern (track 64) long-billed larks; Short-clawed Lark (track 65)

NOTE Distribution is crucial for identification as plumage coloration depends on the colour of the local soil.

Eastern Long-billed Lark
Certhilauda semitorquata
Grasveldlangbeklewerik

Short-clawed Lark
Certhilauda chuana
Kortkloulewerik

long tail

long tail

Length 18 cm **Weight** 40 g
Habitat Grassland in hilly areas, particularly in short grass on stony ground.
Habits Forages mainly alone or in pairs.

TRACK **64**

Call A piercing descending whistle, given either when perched or in display flight.
Comparative track 165

Length 19 cm **Weight** 35 g
Habitat Grassland with scattered small bushes.
Habits Runs in short bursts, like a pipit.

TRACK **65**

Call A piercing fluty whistle, similar in tone to a person whistling, given either when perched or in display flight. Also a series of whistles and liquid trills similar to those of a rock-thrush.
Comparative track 165

AT A GLANCE

✔ Long tail
✔ Habitat
✔ Distribution

Similar-looking species Cape (page 62), Agulhas (page 62), Karoo (page 63) and Benguela (page 63) long-billed larks; Short-clawed Lark (page 64)

Similar-sounding species Cape (track 60), Agulhas (track 61), Karoo (track 62) and Benguela (track 63) long-billed larks; Short-clawed Lark (track 65)

NOTE Distribution is crucial for identification as plumage coloration depends on the colour of the local soil.

AT A GLANCE

✔ Long tail
✔ Habitat
✔ Distribution

Similar-looking species Cape (page 62), Agulhas (page 62), Karoo (page 63), Benguela (page 63) and Eastern (page 64) long-billed larks; Sabota Lark (page 72)

Similar-sounding species Cape (track 60), Agulhas (track 61), Karoo (track 62), Benguela (track 63) and Eastern (page 64) long-billed larks

NOTE Among long-billed larks, the distribution of Eastern Long-billed Lark is the only one to overlap with that of this species. Differences in habitat and call will help to distinguish between them.

Spike-heeled Lark
Chersomanes albofasciata
Vlaktelewerik

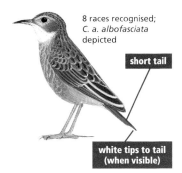

8 races recognised;
C. a. albofasciata
depicted

short tail

**white tips to tail
(when visible)**

Length 14 cm **Weight** 25 g
Habitat Patchy grassland to karoo scrub, where vegetation is sparse.
Habits Usually in smallish groups. Runs at a crouch when disturbed.

  TRACK 66 **Call** A rapid series of soft chuckling sounds, very low in volume, similar to that of Green Wood-Hoopoe.
Comparative track 165

AT A GLANCE

✔ Short tail
✔ White tips to tail (when visible)
✔ Call

Similar-looking species None (the short, white-tipped tail is distinctive)

Similar-sounding species None

NOTE Back colour varies from rufous to grey in different races. The white tips to the tail can be difficult to see, especially when the bird is perched or on the ground, but the short tail is diagnostic within this group.

Typical habitats for this visual group

Karoo scrub is home to all of the species in this group, except Eastern Long-billed and Short-clawed larks.

Grassland with scattered bushes in the dry North West Province is ideal habitat for the Short-clawed Lark.

Karoo Lark
Calendulauda albescens
Karoolewerik

Barlow's Lark
Calendulauda barlowi
Barlowse Lewerik

streaked back

longish bill

streaked flanks

lightly streaked back

heavy bill

unstreaked flanks

Length 17 cm **Weight** 28 g
Habitat Coastal and arid scrub, usually on soft soils or stony ground.
Habits In pairs, defending territory year round. When disturbed, either runs away or gives alarm call from a perch.

 TRACK **67** **Call** A more varied range of *chip* notes than in Dune Lark or Barlow's Lark, and a longer and more complex, swallow-like gurgle.
Comparative track 166

Length 18 cm **Weight** 29 g
Habitat Sparsely vegetated shrubland and grassy dunes; often associated with euphorbia succulents.
Habits In pairs. Most active in early morning, sheltering in shade during the day.

TRACK **68** **Call** A series of 6–9 *chip* notes followed by a swallow-like trill (the shortest within the group).
Comparative track 166

AT A GLANCE
✔ Streaked flanks
✔ Streaked back
✔ Longish bill

 Similar-looking species None (the heavy streaking on the flanks is distinctive)

 Similar-sounding species Barlow's (track 68), Red (track 69), Dune (track 70) and Large-billed (track 81) larks

NOTE The ranges of this species and Barlow's Lark overlap near Port Nolloth, where some hybridisation does occur. Races vary in colour from rich brown to grey.

AT A GLANCE
✔ Unstreaked flanks
✔ Lightly streaked back
✔ Heavy bill

 Similar-looking species Karoo (page 66), Red (page 67) and Dune (page 67) larks

 Similar-sounding species Karoo (track 67), Red (track 69), Dune (track 70) and Large-billed (track 81) larks

NOTE The ranges of this species and Karoo Lark overlap near Port Nolloth, where some hybridisation does occur. Birds in the north are plain above, resembling Dune Lark.

Red Lark
Calendulauda burra
Rooilewerik

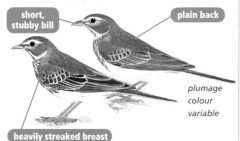

short, stubby bill

plain back

plumage colour variable

heavily streaked breast

Length 19 cm **Weight** 37 g
Habitat Dunes with grass cover.
Habits Usually in pairs. Runs between grass patches or flies to a perch when disturbed. Calls most often in the early morning.

TRACK **69** **Call** One of the longest and most complex in the group, starting with a series of rattles followed by a fast jumbled phrase and ending with a gurgled warble.
Comparative track 166

Dune Lark
Calendulauda erythrochlamys
Duinlewerik

plain back

long, slender bill

faintly streaked breast

Length 17 cm **Weight** 28 g
Habitat Namib dunes with grasses.
Habits Usually in small groups. Runs across open ground between patches of grass.

TRACK **70** **Call** The softest, thinnest and longest in the group. Eight or more widowbird-like chirps followed by a soft, swallow-like gurgle.
Comparative track 166

AT A GLANCE

✔ Plain back
✔ Heavily streaked breast
✔ Short, stubby bill

 Similar-looking species Karoo (page 66), Barlow's (page 66) and Dune (page 67) larks

 Similar-sounding species Karoo (track 67), Barlow's (track 68), Dune (track 70) and Large-billed (track 81) larks

AT A GLANCE

✔ Plain back
✔ Faintly streaked breast
✔ Long, slender bill

 Similar-looking species Barlow's (page 66) and Red (page 67) larks, but the faint breast streaking should distinguish it.

 Similar-sounding species Karoo (track 67), Barlow's (track 68), Red (track 69) and Large-billed (track 81) larks

Fawn-coloured Lark
Calendulauda africanoides
Vaalbruinlewerik

heavily streaked back

short, pointed bill

unstreaked flanks

Length 15 cm **Weight** 23 g
Habitat A range of woodland, particularly on sandy soils and extending to dune habitats in the Northern Cape.
Habits Walks in open patches between grass tufts and bushes. Male calls from a perch.

 TRACK 71 **Call** Includes a jumbled twittering phrase that speeds up across the call. Very similar to that of Cape Grassbird but flutier and less harsh.

AT A GLANCE

✔ Heavily streaked back
✔ Unstreaked flanks
✔ Short, pointed bill
✔ Call

 Similar-looking species None (the short, pointed bill is distinctive)

 Similar-sounding species None

NOTE The contrast between the sandy upper-parts and the white underparts is more striking than in other members of this group. May resemble pale-bellied Rufous-Naped Lark, but is smaller, with smaller bill, and uniformly coloured crown and nape.

 ## Monotonous Lark
Mirafra passerina
Bosveldlewerik

heavily mottled back

conspicuous pale throat

buff breast band with streaks

Length 14 cm **Weight** 24 g
Habitat A range of woodland, avoiding arid areas.
Habits Reclusive and silent, and thus difficult to locate when not breeding.

 TRACK 72 **Call** Liquid, bubbly and rhythmical, with some phrases similar to those of a bee-eater call and others more like that of a Cinnamon-breasted Bunting. Repeats the same phrase monotonously.

AT A GLANCE

✔ Heavily mottled back
✔ Conspicuous pale throat
✔ Buff breast band with streaks
✔ Call

 Similar-looking species None (the buff breast band and white throat are distinctive)

 Similar-sounding species None

Red-capped Lark
Calandrella cinerea
Rooikoplewerik

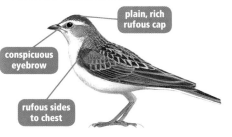

plain, rich rufous cap

conspicuous eyebrow

rufous sides to chest

Length 15 cm **Weight** 24 g
Habitat A range of grassland habitats, but most regularly in ploughed and burned fields.
Habits Forages in large groups. May raise crest when alarmed.

TRACK 73 **Call** A jumble of phrases, the most characteristic being a descending whistle comprising two notes very close together, with a trill on the second note. Mimicry is often included, especially during the high display flight.
Comparative track 162

✔ Plain, rich rufous cap
✔ Rufous sides to chest
✔ Conspicuous eyebrow

 Similar-looking species None, although the juvenile resembles Sclater's Lark (page 73)

 Similar-sounding species Botha's (track 56) and Pink-billed (track 59) larks

NOTE With its brown cap and shoulder and 'tear drop' below the eye, the juvenile resembles Sclater's Lark.

Dusky Lark
Pinarocorys nigricans
Donkerlewerik

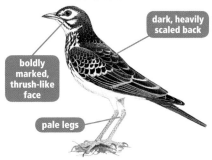

dark, heavily scaled back

boldly marked, thrush-like face

pale legs

Length 20 cm **Weight** 39 g
Habitat Dry savanna and broad-leaved woodland, particularly along gravel roads and around cattle and game.
Habits Often solitary or in small groups. When walking, stops, flicks wings and continues.

TRACK 74 **Call** A shrill *preeea*, similar to a referee's whistle, but this is seldom heard in southern Africa. When here, the birds generally give soft, less diagnostic calls.

✔ Dark, heavily scaled back
✔ Boldly marked, thrush-like face
✔ Pale legs
✔ Call

 Similar-looking species None (the dark back, boldly marked face and pale legs are distinctive)

 Similar-sounding species None

NOTE The juvenile is similar to the adult but has a plain back. A summer migrant (October to May).

Eastern Clapper Lark
Mirafra fasciolata
Hoëveldklappertjie

only separable on call and distribution

Length 15 cm **Weight** 30 g
Habitat Tall grassland, either open or with scattered bushes.
Habits Difficult to flush; when disturbed, prefers to run but may perch in open.

TRACK
75
Call A wing rattle of constant speed culminating in an ascending, drawn-out whistle, given as the bird flies upward in display and then drops back to the ground.
Comparative track 167

Cape Clapper Lark
Mirafra apiata
Kaapse Klappertjie

only separable on call and distribution

M. a. apiata   *M. a. marjoriae* (extreme southern distribution)

Length 13 cm **Weight** 28 g
Habitat Dense bush and fynbos. Sometimes in cropland near suitable habitat.
Habits Difficult to flush; when flushed, prefers to run but may perch in open before dropping down into denser vegetation.

TRACK
76
Call An accelerating wing rattle that culminates in an ascending or floaty whistle, given during the display flight.
Comparative track 167

AT A GLANCE

✔ Habitat
✔ Distribution
✔ Call

Similar-looking species Cape Clapper (p. 70) and Flappet (p.71) larks

Similar-sounding species Cape Clapper Lark (track 76); Flappet Lark (track 77)

NOTE Distribution plays an important role in separating clapper larks.

AT A GLANCE

✔ Habitat
✔ Distribution
✔ Call

Similar-looking species Eastern Clapper (p. 70) and Flappet (p.71) larks

Similar-sounding species Eastern Clapper Lark (track 75); Flappet Lark (track 77)

NOTE Distribution plays an important role when separating clapper larks.

Flappet Lark
Mirafra rufocinnamomea
Laeveldklappertjie

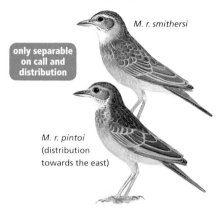

M. r. smithersi

only separable on call and distribution

M. r. pintoi
(distribution towards the east)

Length 14 cm **Weight** 26 g
Habitat Grassy clearings and gravel roads in mostly broad-leaved but also acacia woodland.
Habits Remains hidden when not displaying, and difficult to flush. In display flight, male claps wings together to produce a rattling sound.

TRACK 77 **Call** One or two short wing rattles followed by a longer one. In ideal conditions, a soft jumbled phrase can be heard at the end of the rattle (in the clapper larks, a piercing whistle concludes the rattle).
Comparative track 167

AT A GLANCE

✔ Habitat
✔ Distribution
✔ Call

 Similar-looking species Eastern (p. 70) and Cape (p. 70) clapper larks and Rufous-naped Lark (p. 74)

 Similar-sounding species Eastern (track 75) and Cape (track 76) clapper larks

NOTE Visually similar to the clapper larks, but habitat and call help to separate them. Birds tend to be darkest towards the east of their distribution.

Typical habitats for this visual group

Tall grassland with scattered bushes is the favoured home of the Eastern Clapper Lark.

The Cape Clapper Lark is best located in habitats with dense bush and fynbos.

Gravel roads in predominantly broad-leaved woodland might reveal a Flappet Lark.

Melodious Lark
Mirafra cheniana
Spotlewerik

rufous in flight feathers

short, stubby bill

streaked buff breast band

Length 12 cm **Weight** 20 g
Habitat *Rooigras*-dominated grassland, where grass is short and patchy.
Habits Inconspicuous unless singing, which it usually does in flight. Difficult to flush.

TRACK 78 Call A continuous stream of musical notes and mimicry with very short gaps between phrases. Similar to that of Sabota Lark but lacks the piercing introductory notes. Some calls have a three- or four-noted phrase structure similar to that of reed-warblers.
Comparative track 168

Sabota Lark

Calendulauda sabota
Sabotalewerik

small size

no rufous in flight feathers

C. s. sabota

C. s. bradfieldi
(arid south-western form)

pale to very pale belly

Length 14 cm **Weight** 25 g
Habitat Open acacia woodland to Karoo scrub, where it occurs among larger bushes.
Habits Often perches, usually on a nearby bush when flushed.

TRACK 79 Call Short phrases with some mimicry, usually with piercing introductory notes that have an easily recognisable tone. Similar to the call of Melodious Lark but with longer pauses between phrases.
Comparative track 168

AT A GLANCE

✔ Streaked buff breast band
✔ Short, stubby bill
✔ Rufous in flight feathers

 Similar-looking species None (the rufous edges to the wing panel and short bill are distinctive)

 Similar-sounding species Sabota Lark (track 79)

AT A GLANCE

✔ Small size
✔ Pale to very pale belly
✔ No rufous in flight feathers

 Similar-looking species None

 Similar-sounding species Melodious Lark (track 78)

Sclater's Lark
Spizocorys sclateri
Namakwalewerik

small size

no rufous in flight feathers

rich buff belly

Length 13 cm **Weight** 20 g
Habitat Arid areas with small bushes, usually on quartzitic soil.
Habits Walks slowly when foraging. Inconspicuous except at water, where it occurs in large groups.

TRACK 80 **Call** Jumbled, with *purp* notes like those of a European Bee-eater and short chirps intermediate between those of a warbler and a sparrow.
Comparative track 164

Large-billed Lark
Galerida magnirostris
Dikbeklewerik

large size

no rufous in flight feathers

pale belly

Length 18 cm **Weight** 43 g
Habitat Arid areas, from fynbos to dry grassland.
Habits Walks slowly when foraging. Sometimes occurs in groups of up to 25 birds. Flies some distance when flushed, but easily located when vocal.

TRACK 81 **Call** In two parts: a single-noted click followed by a full, fluty and almost comical jumbled whistle.
Comparative track 166

AT A GLANCE
✔ Small size
✔ Rich buff belly
✔ No rufous in flight feathers

Similar-looking species None

Similar-sounding species Tractrac Chat (track 95)

NOTE This species also has a heavy and distinctive, almost upward-pointing bill that may cause confusion with Large-billed Lark.

AT A GLANCE
✔ Large size
✔ Pale belly
✔ No rufous in flight feathers

Similar-looking species None

Similar-sounding species Karoo (track 67), Barlow's (track 68), Red (track 69) and Dune (track 70) larks

NOTE Be aware that the large size and heavy bill of Rufous-naped Lark may cause confusion with this species.

Rufous-naped Lark
Mirafra africana
Rooineklewerik

rufous
in flight feathers

large, heavy
bill

large size

Length 17 cm **Weight** 42 g
Habitat Ranges from grassland to woodland, with the exception of dense grassland.
Habits Inconspicuous in winter, but sings prominently from perches in summer. Difficult to flush.

 TRACK **82**

Call Distinctive but highly variable, comprising three or four piercing whistles such as *tri-lee-tri-loo* or *tree-ri-loo*. Sometimes also a wing rattle.

AT A GLANCE

✔ Large size
✔ Large, heavy bill
✔ Rufous in flight feathers
✔ Call

 Similar-looking species Eastern Clapper Lark (page 70)

Similar-sounding species None

NOTE Crown more richly coloured than nape, giving a capped appearance. This, with larger size and heavy bill separates it from Eastern Clapper, Flappet and Fawn-coloured larks.

Typical habitats for this visual group

Grassland is ideal habitat for the Melodious Lark and the very vocal Rufous-naped Lark.

Within this group, the Sabota Lark is the only species to be found in acacia woodland.

Karoo scrub, particularly in the drier areas, is ideal habitat for both Sclater's and Large-billed larks. Also look out for the larger-billed Bradfield's race of Sabota Lark.

Flycatchers

The grey-brown flycatchers are small, dull birds with very few distinctive markings. The presence of rictal bristles (whiskers at the base of the bill) separates flycatchers from other LBJ families, notably chats, but the bristles are often difficult to see. The plain tail of birds in this family is more reliable as a distinguishing feature from wheatears, chats and honeyguides, all of which have a striking tail pattern and sometimes also a rump that is colourful or clearly marked. Noticeably short legs are another flycatcher characteristic, and, even though the legs of the Chat Flycatcher are somewhat longer, they are still shorter than those of regular chats.

Flycatcher calls are simple, comprising scratchy notes and soft whistles.

The birds are often seen on a prominent, relatively low and usually covered perch, from which they hawk insects in flight or, like the Marico, Pale and Chat flycatchers, take them on the ground before returning to their original position. Their motionless, upright stance while perched contrasts with the more horizontal feeding posture of chats and wheatears.

LOOK FOR

- ✔ overall grey-brown coloration
- ✔ head markings
- ✔ underpart coloration and presence or absence of streaking on chest
- ✔ plain tail
- ✔ hawking behaviour

FLYCATCHERS HAVE ONLY ONE VISUAL GROUP

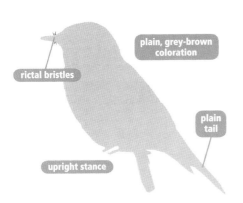

rictal bristles

plain, grey-brown coloration

plain tail

upright stance

Spotted Flycatcher

Typical habitats for this visual group

Open woodland, particularly with a clear understorey (such as camp and picnic sites) is ideal for the Spotted Flycatcher.

Sparsely covered grassland in the drier west of the region is a good place to search for the rather bulky Chat Flycatcher.

The Marico Flycatcher is one of the more common species found in acacia woodland, although Spotted and Pale flycatchers may also occur here.

Chat Flycatcher
Bradornis infuscatus
Grootvlieëvanger

pale throat

same size as a thrush

warm, soft brown wash to underparts

Length 20 cm **Weight** 37 g
Habitat Open woodland to sparsely covered grassland.
Habits Solitary or in pairs, occasionally in small groups. Hawks insects from a perch, taking large portions of its food from the ground.

TRACK 83 **Call** A series of warbler-like notes, similar to the soft clucks of the Helmeted Guineafowl. Also a series of rapidly repeated, sparrow-like *chirup* sounds.
Comparative track 170

AT A GLANCE

✔ Warm, soft brown wash to underparts
✔ Pale throat
✔ Same size as a thrush

Similar-looking species Pale Flycatcher (page 77)

Similar-sounding species Pale Flycatcher

NOTE Juveniles are streaked only on the chest and flanks. The flight feathers of juveniles and adults have buff edges.

Marico Flycatcher
Bradornis mariquensis
Maricovlieëvanger

rich sandy-brown upperparts

contrasting light underparts

smaller than a thrush

Length 18 cm **Weight** 24 g
Habitat Drier areas with acacia woodland and savanna.
Habits Solitary or in pairs, sometimes in small groups. Hawks insects from a perch, taking large portions of its food from the ground.

 Call Similar to that of the House Sparrow but including some high-pitched, typical flycatcher *tseeep* notes.

TRACK 84

Pale Flycatcher
Bradornis pallidus
Muiskleurvlieëvanger

pale grey-brown upperparts

off-white (dirty-looking) underparts

smaller than a thrush

Length 16 cm **Weight** 22 g
Habitat Forest, acacia and miombo woodland and bushveld.
Habits Solitary or in pairs. Territorial. Hawks insects from a perch, taking large portions of its food from the ground. Flicks tail when landing.

Call A series of excited, weaver-like 'swizzling' sounds, similar to those of the Village Weaver.
Comparative track 170

Spotted Flycatcher
Muscicapa striata
Europese Vlieëvanger

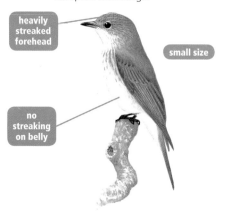

heavily streaked forehead

small size

no streaking on belly

Length 14 cm **Weight** 15 g
Habitat Woodland and gardens where the understorey is open.
Habits Solitary or sometimes in pairs. Hawks insects from a perch.

TRACK 85 Call A sharp *tsee-chik* and a very high-pitched, short but descending *tseeee*.
Comparative track 169

AT A GLANCE

✔ Heavily streaked forehead
✔ Small size
✔ No streaking on belly

 Similar-looking species None (the streaking on the head is distinctive)

 Similar-sounding species African Dusky Flycatcher (track 86)

NOTE The head shape is more sloped than that of African Dusky Flycatcher, and the overall coloration browner. A summer migrant (October to April).

African Dusky Flycatcher
Muscicapa adusta
Donkervlieëvanger

plain forehead

small size

indistinct streaking on underparts

Length 13 cm **Weight** 11 g
Habitat Dense areas of montane and lowland forest.
Habits Usually solitary. Hawks insects from a perch, occasionally flicking its wings while perched.

TRACK 86 Call A high-pitched, descending *tseeeee* and a distinctive *tsip-ree-ree-ree*, rising in pitch and with a metallic tone.
Comparative track 169

AT A GLANCE

✔ Plain forehead
✔ Small size
✔ Indistinct streaking on underparts

 Similar-looking species None

 Similar-sounding species Spotted Flycatcher (track 85)

NOTE The head shape is more rounded than that of Spotted Flycatcher, and the overall coloration is more blue-grey.

Scrub-Robins

SEPARATING VISUAL GROUPS

Scrub-robins have a typical 'robin' build, but they are browner and more cryptic in appearance than the robin-chats and lack the robin-chats' more vivid coloration. Their tails tend to be more richly coloured, however, and in all species end in white tips. They are often held erect or flicked slowly up and down. The bold facial markings of scrub-robins help to identify them as a group, making them unlikely to be confused with any other group, except perhaps chats and wheatears. However, the robin-chats' more secretive behaviour and the combination of tail-flicking and strong facial and wing markings should distinguish them.

Scrub-robin calls are melodic and range from repetitive to musical.

The birds forage on the ground, usually within dense vegetation.

LOOK FOR

- ✔ wing bars
- ✔ rump coloration
- ✔ tail coloration and markings
- ✔ chest and/or belly coloration and markings
- ✔ presence of a malar stripe

SCRUB-ROBINS HAVE ONLY ONE VISUAL GROUP

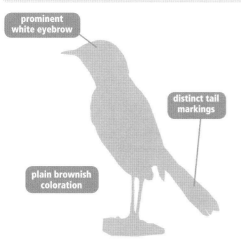

prominent white eyebrow

distinct tail markings

plain brownish coloration

White-browed Scrub-Robin

Brown Scrub-Robin
Cercotrichas signata
Bruinwipstert

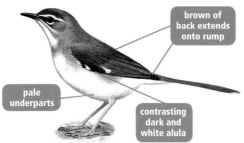

brown of back extends onto rump

pale underparts

contrasting dark and white alula

Length 19 cm **Weight** 35 g
Habitat Moist coastal, mistbelt and riverine forest.
Habits Usually solitary. Shy, moves around in leaf litter on the ground.

TRACK 87 **Call** A mournful whistle, with some typical robin *chuck* notes and some high-pitched trills.

AT A GLANCE

✔ Brown of back extends onto rump
✔ Contrasting dark and white alula
✔ Pale underparts
✔ Call

Similar-looking species None (the combination of brown rump and pale flanks is distinctive)

Similar-sounding species None

NOTE The dark and white alula should not be confused with the double white wing bar of White-browed Scrub-Robin.

Karoo Scrub-Robin
Cercotrichas coryphoeus
Slangverklikker

grey-brown of back extends onto rump

dark underparts

plain wing

Length 17 cm **Weight** 19 g
Habitat Usually open ground among low Karoo bushes.
Habits Often in pairs. Forages on the ground, running or hopping over the open ground between bushes.

TRACK 88 **Call** A series of sparrow- and warbler-like notes (the most warbler-like of all scrub-robin calls).

AT A GLANCE

✔ Grey-brown of back extends onto rump
✔ Plain wing
✔ Dark underparts
✔ Call

Similar-looking species None (the combination of brown rump and brown flanks is distinctive)

Similar-sounding species None

Kalahari Scrub-Robin
Cercotrichas paena
Kalahariwipstert

no malar stripe

no wing bar

rufous rump and tail

Length 16 cm **Weight** 20 g
Habitat Drier areas, particularly sandveld, moving on bare ground and in open areas with scrub.
Habits Solitary or in pairs. Forages on the ground.

TRACK 89 **Call** A series of varied whistles, chirps and other typical robin sounds, usually including a distinctive *see-seeooo, see-seeeooo*.

White-browed Scrub-Robin
Cercotrichas leucophrys
Gestreepte Wipstert

double white wing bar

C. l. leucophrys

C. l. ovamboensis

Length 15 cm **Weight** 20 g
Habitat Varied woodland, including savanna, acacia and miombo.
Habits In pairs. Forages on the ground, usually under cover of vegetation.

TRACK 90 **Call** Bubbly and musical, with bulbul- or thrush-like characteristics, as well as typical robin whistles and trills.

Chats & wheatears

Chats in general are dull brown or pale birds with strongly patterned tails, as are the non-breeding wheatears (Pied, Northern and Isabelline) that occur in southern Africa as vagrants and the juvenile Capped Wheatear. Although similar in some respects to flycatchers, chats have noticeably longer legs and their tail markings and rump colour are distinctive. Separating some members of this group can be tricky, and it helps to concentrate on tail and rump colour and markings. Underwing colour also plays an important role in identifying species and, although this is often difficult to discern, persistence and careful attention to this feature will pay dividends. A series of photographs taken as a bird is flying off can help to determine underwing colour.

Unlike flycatchers, chats and wheatears forage on the ground, although they may perch prominently at the top of a low bush or on a post. Some species habitually flick their wings.

Although some chat calls are distinctive, many are not and a number of species are best identified visually. Note that the migrant wheatears (Pied, Northern and Isabelline) and the Whinchat are extremely rare vagrants.

LOOK FOR

✔ tail coloration/ markings
✔ lower back coloration (including number of colours)
✔ underpart and underwing coloration
✔ relative wing projection
✔ facial markings
✔ size

Juvenile Capped Wheatear

CHATS & WHEATEARS CAN BE DIVIDED INTO THREE VISUAL GROUPS

Large size, rump white (page 84)

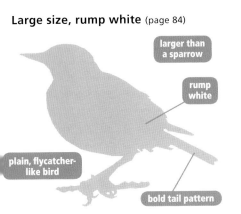

larger than a sparrow

rump white

plain, flycatcher-like bird

bold tail pattern

Small chats (page 90)

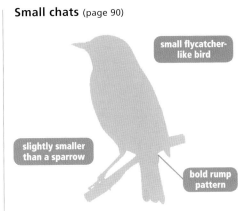

small flycatcher-like bird

slightly smaller than a sparrow

bold rump pattern

Large size, rump not white (page 88)

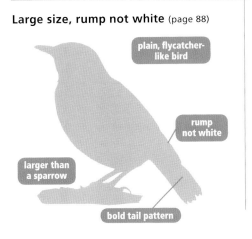

plain, flycatcher-like bird

rump not white

larger than a sparrow

bold tail pattern

Whinchat

Pied Wheatear
(female & non-breeding male)

Oenanthe pleschanka

Bontskaapwagter

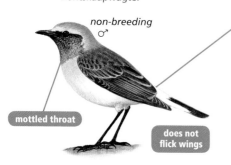

non-breeding ♂

mottled throat

does not flick wings

two-tone lower back (light brown and white)

♀

does not flick wings

comparatively long tail and short wing projection

Length 15 cm; **Tail** 5.3–6.3 cm (female); **Wing** 8.5–9.8 cm (female) **Weight** 20 g

Habitat Stony arid regions with scattered scrub and trees.

Habits Usually solitary. Perches on trees and bushes, but hawks insects from the ground.

TRACK **91**

Call A piercing mix of typical wheatear warbles and mimicry, with a canary-like quality. Best identified visually.

Female

AT A GLANCE

FEMALE

✔ Two-tone lower back (light brown and white)

✔ Does not flick wings

✔ Comparatively long tail and short wing projection

NON-BREEDING MALE

✔ Two-tone lower back (light brown and white)

✔ Does not flick wings

✔ Mottled throat

 Similar-looking species Capped Wheatear, juvenile (page 85); Northern Wheatear, female (page 86); Isabelline Wheatear (page 86)

 Similar-sounding species Capped (track 92), Northern (track 94) and Isabelline (track 93) wheatears; Buff-streaked Chat (track 98)

NOTE Female Northern and Pied wheatears are very difficult to separate, and the relative wing and tail lengths provide the best clue. A very rare vagrant.

Capped Wheatear (juvenile)
Oenanthe pileata
Hoëveldskaapwagter

does not flick wings

three-tone lower back (light brown, buff and white)

grey to dark underwing coverts

Length 17 cm **Weight** 25 g
Habitat Ranges from short grassland to semi-arid areas and cropland. Also found on recently burned land.
Habits Usually solitary or in pairs, sometimes in groups. Often perches on mounds, posts or stones. Forages mainly on the ground. Monogamous breeder.

TRACK 92 **Call** A piercing mix of typical wheatear warbles and mimicry, with a very scratchy and warbler-like quality. Best identified visually.

Juvenile

AT A GLANCE
✔ Three-tone lower back (light brown, buff and white)
✔ Does not flick wings
✔ Grey to dark underwing coverts

 Similar-looking species Northern Wheatear, female & non-breeding male (page 86); Pied Wheatear, female (page 84); Isabelline Wheatear (page 86)

Similar-sounding species Northern (track 94), Pied (track 91) and Isabelline (track 93) wheatears; Buff-streaked Chat (track 98)

Isabelline Wheatear
Oenanthe isabellina
Isabellaskaapwagter

three-tone lower back: dull brown, rich brown and white

does not flick wings

pale to white underwing coverts

Length 16 cm **Weight** 30 g
Habitat Semi-arid areas with low bushes or scattered trees.
Habits Usually solitary. Perches prominently but forages on the ground, often raising its wings as it darts after prey and then revealing its underwing coverts.

TRACK 93 **Call** A piercing mix of typical wheatear warbles and mimicry, with a canary-like quality. Best identified visually.

AT A GLANCE

✔ Three-tone lower back: dull brown, rich brown and white
✔ Does not flick wings
✔ Pale to white underwing coverts

 Similar-looking species Capped Wheatear, juvenile (page 85); Northern Wheatear, female (page 86); Pied Wheatear, female (page 84)

 Similar-sounding species Capped (track 92), Northern (track 94) and Pied (track 91) wheatears; Buff-streaked Chat (track 98)

NOTE A very rare vagrant.

Northern Wheatear
(female & non-breeding male)
Oenanthe oenanthe
Europese Skaapwagter

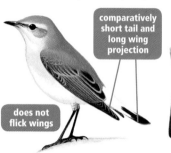

comparatively short tail and long wing projection

does not flick wings

two-tone lower back: light brown and white

Length 15 cm; tail 4.7–6.3 cm; wing 9.1–10.4 cm **Weight** 25 g
Habitat Dry areas with short grass, degraded woodland and the vicinity of rural settlements.
Habits Usually solitary and may be territorial, even on migration.

TRACK 94 **Call** A piercing mix of typical wheatear warbles and mimicry, with a canary-like quality; more piercing and less canary-like than that of Pied Wheatear. Best identified visually.

AT A GLANCE

✔ Two-tone lower back: light brown and white
✔ Does not flick wings
✔ Comparatively short tail and long wing projection

 Similar-looking species Capped Wheatear, juvenile (page 85); Pied Wheatear, female (page 84); Isabelline Wheatear (page 86)

 Similar-sounding species Capped (track 92), Pied (track 91) and Isabelline (track 93) wheatears; Buff-streaked Chat (track 98)

NOTE Female Northern and Pied wheatears are very difficult to separate, and the relative wing and tail lengths provide the best clue. A rare vagrant.

Karoo Chat (pale form)
Cercomela schlegelii namaquensis
Karoospekvreter

two-tone lower back: pale grey and white

flicks wings infrequently

dark triangle on tail

Length 17 cm **Weight** 32 g
Habitat Dwarf shrubland in dry areas.
Habits Often perches in the open. Flicks wings infrequently and usually only once.

Call Five scratchy notes, like counting *one-two-three-four-five*, with three and four at a slightly higher pitch. Similar to that of Common Myna.

Tractrac Chat
Cercomela tractrac
Woestynspekvreter

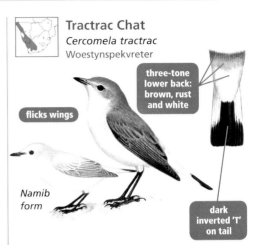

three-tone lower back: brown, rust and white

flicks wings

Namib form

dark inverted 'T' on tail

Length 14 cm **Weight** 20 g
Habitat Arid regions on open plains with grass and small bushes. Also dune shrubland.
Habits Perches in the open and flicks wings (but less than Familiar Chat). Easily disturbed and can be difficult to approach.

 TRACK **95** **Call** An excited jumble of typical chat chirps, notes similar to those of South African Cliff-Swallow, and kestrel-like descending notes.

AT A GLANCE

✔ Two-tone lower back: pale grey and white
✔ Dark triangle on tail
✔ Flicks wings infrequently
✔ Call

 Similar-looking species Tractrac Chat (page 87)

 Similar-sounding species None

NOTE Some dark-form Karoo Chats (page 89) have pale grey uppertail coverts and may be inadvertently placed in this group. Nevertheless, heeding the pointers will produce a correct identification. Most of the tail is dark, with only a very narrow, tapering white edge.

AT A GLANCE

✔ Three-tone lower back: brown, rust and white
✔ Flicks wings
✔ Dark inverted 'T' on tail

 Similar-looking species Karoo Chat (page 87)

 Similar-sounding species Sclater's Lark (track 80)

NOTE The western race is very pale. Capped, Isabelline, Pied and Northern wheatears also have the inverted 'T' on the tail.

Sickle-winged Chat
Cercomela sinuata
Vlaktespekvreter

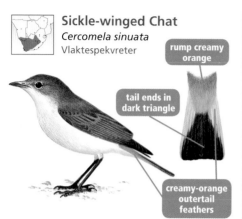

rump creamy orange

tail ends in dark triangle

creamy-orange outertail feathers

Length 15 cm **Weight** 19 g
Habitat Ranges from Karoo scrub to bushy mountain slopes.
Habits Perches in the open. Flies from bush to bush and flicks wings more readily than Karoo Chat, usually twice.

TRACK 96 **Call** A range of sounds, including *preeu-preeu* (like a budgerigar) and *chik-chik-chik-trrrr* (like Rattling Cisticola).

AT A GLANCE

✔ Rump creamy orange
✔ Tail ends in dark triangle
✔ Creamy-orange outertail feathers

Similar-looking species Familiar Chat (page 88)

Similar-sounding species Rattling Cisticola (track 47)

NOTE The more pronounced white eye-ring and the buff edging to the wing coverts help to separate this species from Familiar Chat.

Familiar Chat
Cercomela familiaris
Gewone Spekvreter

rump bright rufous

tail bright rufous

dark inverted 'T' on tail extends to rump

Length 15 cm **Weight** 22 g
Habitat Rocky and hilly areas in open woodland, extending into Karoo. Also gardens.
Habits Habituated to human presence and often found around picnic sites. Flicks wings a number of times after landing.

TRACK 97 **Call** A distinctive *chirp-chit-chit* sequence. Also a series of warbler-like notes interspersed with a scratchy sound, like grinding teeth.

AT A GLANCE

✔ Rump bright rufous
✔ Tail bright rufous
✔ Dark inverted 'T' on tail extends to rump
✔ Call

Similar-looking species Sickle-winged Chat (page 88)

Similar-sounding species None

NOTE The less pronounced white eye-ring and lack of buff edging to the wing coverts help to separate this species from Sickle-winged Chat.

Buff-streaked Chat (female)
Oenanthe bifasciata
Bergklipwagter

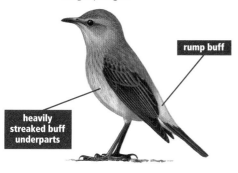

rump buff

heavily streaked buff underparts

Length 17 cm **Weight** 33 g
Habitat Rocky parts of montane grassland and near rural settlements.
Habits Solitary, in pairs or in small groups. Shy, but often seen prominently perched some distance away. Hawks insects as well as forages on the ground.

TRACK 98 **Call** A rich mix of full-sounding warbles and mimicry.

✔ Rump buff
✔ Heavily streaked buff underparts

 Similar-looking species None (the buff rump is distinctive)

 Similar-sounding species Capped (track 92), Isabelline (track 93), Pied (track 91) and Northern (Track 94) wheatears

NOTE Although the male has a white rump, his other markings are distinctive enough to make confusion with other chats unlikely.

Karoo Chat (dark form)
Cercomela schlegelii excluding subspecies *namaquensis*
Karoospekvreter

rump uniform grey or two-tone pale and dark grey

Length 17 cm **Weight** 32 g
Habitat Dwarf shrubland in Karoo, seldom venturing into gardens.
Habits Often perches in the open. Flicks wings infrequently and usually only once.

Call Five scratchy notes, like counting *one-two-three-four-five*, with three and four at a slightly higher pitch. Similar to that of Common Myna.

✔ Rump uniform grey or two-tone pale and dark grey
✔ Call

 Similar-looking species None (the grey rump is distinctive)

 Similar-sounding species None

NOTE Some dark-form Karoo Chats have pale grey uppertail coverts that may be mistaken for a white rump, placing the bird in the wrong visual group (see also pale-form Karoo Chat, page 87). Nevertheless, the pointers will produce a correct identification. Most of the tail is dark, with only a very narrow, tapering white edge.

African Stonechat (female)
Saxicola torquatus
Gewone Bontrokkie

Whinchat
(female & non-breeding male)
Saxicola rubetra
Europese Bontrokkie

white rump

brown rump with black streaks

♀
and non-breeding

Length 14 cm **Weight** 15 g
Habitat Grassy slopes, grassland with bushes, edges of forest and wetland.
Habits Perches in the open and often flicks its tail and wings in typical chat fashion. Very rarely forages on the ground (as Whinchat does), preferring to hawk insects.

TRACK 99 **Call** A series of canary-like trills and warbles. Contact and alarm call is a distinctive *tseeet-tchik-tchik* or a repeated *tchik-tchik*.

Length 13 cm **Weight** 14 g
Habitat Grassland and wetland with suitable perches, as well as wetland and forest edges.
Habits Forages on the ground, hopping rapidly and occasionally running. Perches in the open.

TRACK 100 **Call** Usually silent in Africa. Jumbled canary-like phrases, including some mimicry, and *tik-tik* or *hwee-tik-tik*.

AT A GLANCE
✔ White rump
✔ Call

 Similar-looking species Whinchat, female (page 90)

 Similar-sounding species None

NOTE Juvenile African Stonechat has a brown rump but the rump lacks the black streaks of Whinchat. The mottled plumage of juveniles and unstreaked rump prevent confusion with Whinchat.

AT A GLANCE
✔ Brown rump with black streaks

 Similar-looking species Stonechat, female (page 90)

 Similar-sounding species None

NOTE A rare vagrant. Although juvenile African Stonechat also has a brown rump, the mottled plumage and lack of black streaks on the rump will prevent confusion with Whinchat.

SEPARATING VISUAL GROUPS

Weavers

Weavers are small to medium-sized sparrow-like birds that, being seed-eaters, tend to have strong, stout bills and generally hop as they forage on the ground. In the breeding season the males are mostly brightly coloured and can easily be identified. The females and non-breeding males, however, are duller and less conspicuous in tones of soft brown and green to pale yellow. They are most likely to be confused with female and non-breeding male bishops and their allies and also with canaries. Their coloration is subtly greener than the buff tones of the bishop group, and they are noticeably larger than canaries. In general, it helps to become familiar with the overall shape of weavers compared with other similar seed-eaters.

These species are mainly sedentary, although some are nomadic in response to the availability of food. All species build extravagant woven nests that are either attached to strong reeds over water or hang from the ends of bare branches.

Many weavers utter a distinctive 'swizzling' call, like a nasal buzzing.

LOOK FOR

✔ back colour and/or markings
✔ belly and/or chest coloration
✔ colour of bill, legs and eyes

WEAVERS HAVE ONLY ONE VISUAL GROUP

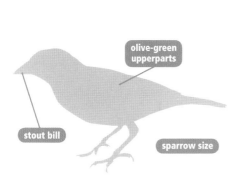

olive-green upperparts

stout bill

sparrow size

Southern Masked-Weaver

Lesser Masked-Weaver
(female & non-breeding male)
Ploceus intermedius
Kleingeelvink

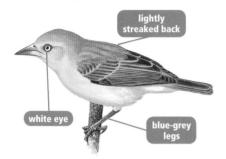

lightly streaked back

white eye

blue-grey legs

Length 14 cm **Weight** 20 g
Habitat Reed beds, woodland and forest.
Habits Occurs mainly in flocks. Forages in trees.

TRACK 101

Call Typical weaver 'swizzling' but as if played at high speed.

AT A GLANCE

✔ Lightly streaked back
✔ White eye
✔ Blue-grey legs
✔ Call

Similar-looking species None (the combination of white eyes and blue-grey legs is distinctive)

Similar-sounding species None

Southern Masked-Weaver
(female & non-breeding male)
Ploceus velatus
Swartkeelgeelvink

greenish back and crown

bill less robust

legs not blue-grey

Length 15 cm **Weight** 33 g
Habitat Open and cultivated areas, woodland, parks and gardens. Associated with water.
Habits Occurs in flocks, gathering at nesting/ roosting areas at dusk.

TRACK 102

Call Typical weaver 'swizzling' but rising and followed by a descending *zeeeeeeoooooo*. Includes raspy chuckles.
Comparative track 171

AT A GLANCE

✔ Streaked greenish back and crown
✔ Legs not blue-grey
✔ Bill less robust

Similar-looking species Village (page 93) and Southern Brown-throated (page 94) weavers

Similar-sounding species Village (track 103) and Cape (track 104) weavers

NOTE The uniform olive wash to the back and crown separates this species from Village Weaver, which has a greyish back.

Village Weaver
(female & non-breeding male)
Ploceus cucullatus
Bontrugwewer

mottled greyish back contrasts with greenish head

heavy bill

legs not blue-grey

Length 16 cm **Weight** 34 g
Habitat Wooded and forested areas, including parks and gardens. Usually associated with water.
Habits Usually occurs in flocks, gathering at nesting/roosting areas at dusk.

TRACK 103 **Call** Typical weaver 'swizzling' but includes what sounds like high-pitched machine-gun fire.
Comparative track 171

AT A GLANCE

✔ Mottled greyish back contrasts with greenish head
✔ Legs not blue-grey
✔ Heavy bill

Similar-looking species Southern Masked-Weaver (page 92); Southern Brown-throated Weaver (page 94)

Similar-sounding species Southern Masked-Weaver (track 102); Cape Weaver (track 104)

NOTE The greyish back and greenish crown separate this species from Southern Masked-Weaver, which has uniform greenish upperparts.

Cape Weaver
(female & non-breeding male)
Ploceus capensis
Kaapse Wewer

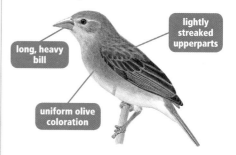

lightly streaked upperparts

long, heavy bill

uniform olive coloration

Length 18 cm **Weight** 46 g
Habitat Open areas with water and small clumps of trees or bushes.
Habits Occurs in flocks, often associating with other weaver species.

TRACK 104 **Call** A series of 'swizzling' notes like a playing card against bicycle spokes speeding up and slowing down.
Comparative track 171

AT A GLANCE

✔ Uniform olive coloration
✔ Lightly streaked upperparts
✔ Long, heavy bill

Similar-looking species None (the olive coloration and comparatively long bill are distinctive)

Similar-sounding species Southern Masked-Weaver (track 102); Village Weaver (track 103)

Red-headed Weaver
(female & non-breeding male)
Anaplectes melanotis
Rooikopwewer

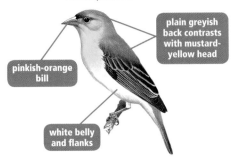

plain greyish back contrasts with mustard-yellow head

pinkish-orange bill

white belly and flanks

Length 14 cm **Weight** 22 g
Habitat Woodland ranging from broad-leaved to acacia and miombo.
Habits Solitary or in pairs. Forages mainly from the ground and will sometimes hawk insects.

TRACK
105

Call A combination of nasal *zeep* and *chirrup* notes like those of Bushveld Pipit and typical weaver 'swizzles' similar to those of Cape Weaver but thinner and at a higher pitch.

Southern Brown-throated Weaver
(female & non-breeding male)
Ploceus xanthopterus
Bruinkeelwewer

heavily streaked back

very heavy bill

cinnamon wash on rump

Length 15 cm **Weight** 24 g
Habitat Mainly reed beds, although it moves to forest and woodland to feed.
Habits In pairs or small flocks, foraging in trees and bushes rather than on the ground.

Call Typical weaver 'swizzling' but includes drawn-out nasal sounds like the soft crying of a baby and some high-pitched canary-like notes.

AT A GLANCE

✔ Plain greyish back contrasts with mustard-yellow head
✔ White belly and flanks
✔ Pinkish-orange bill
✔ Call

Similar-looking species None

Similar-sounding species None

AT A GLANCE

✔ Heavily streaked back
✔ Cinnamon wash on rump
✔ Very heavy bill
✔ Call

Similar-looking species Southern Masked-Weaver (page 92); Village Weaver (page 93)

Similar-sounding species None

Chestnut Weaver
(female & non-breeding male)
Ploceus rubiginosus
Bruinwewer

heavily mottled brown and buff upperparts

dull brown rump

buff wash to underparts

Typical habitats for this visual group

Length 14 cm **Weight** 30 g
Habitat Thornveld and riverine woodland.
Habits Occurs in flocks, foraging mainly on grasses. Breeds colonially, with several hundred nests in one tree.

TRACK 106 **Call** A series of well-spaced, wader-like *cheeeu* notes.

AT A GLANCE

✔ Buff wash to underparts
✔ Heavily mottled brown and buff upperparts
✔ Dull brown rump
✔ Call

 Similar-looking species None (the brown rump and generally brown upperparts are distinctive)

 Similar-sounding species None

NOTE Beware of confusion with female and non-breeding male bishops and widowbirds. Juveniles have a lightly streaked chest.

Weavers occur in a wide range of habitats, from woodland to forest, cultivated lands and even gardens. Some species, like the Chestnut Weaver, are only found in thornveld and riverine woodland. Others, such as the Red-headed Weaver, prefer broad-leaved, acacia and miombo woodlands.

Bishops & allied species

SEPARATING VISUAL GROUPS

Female and non-breeding male bishops and their allies – whydahs and paradise-whydahs, widowbirds, indigobirds, queleas and the Cuckoo Finch – make up a cryptically coloured group of birds that look very similar in varying shades of brown. They are very difficult to separate, with the exception of some non-breeding males that have coloured patches on the shoulder (the colour, yellow or red, is the same as that in their often flamboyant breeding plumage). Underwing coloration can be important, especially among widowbirds. It is not easy to see, but look out for it when the bird takes off: the Fan-tailed Widowbird, for example, often reveals a flash of cinnamon. Similarly, the length of the tail in non-breeding birds can be significant when placing a bird in a visual group. To help you become familiar with the differences in length, even when they are subtle, we have included the relevant measurements for non-breeding birds where appropriate.

Like other seed-eaters, bishops and their allies have strong, conical bills. As a group, they generally have browner and more buff-coloured plumage compared to female and non-breeding weavers, whose coloration is more greenish. When distinguishing between the groups, it helps to become familiar with their overall shape as well as subtle colour differences: members of the bishop family, for instance, appear larger and plumper than canaries.

These species forage on the ground, noticeably hopping as they do so. Unlike weavers, most of them occur almost exclusively in grasslands and wetlands, where they often build their nests in reed beds. The males of this group are mostly polygynous, having several successive mates in the course of a single breeding season. The whydahs, indigobirds and Cuckoo Finch are brood parasites, laying their eggs in other species' nests.

LOOK FOR

- ✔ head markings
- ✔ streaking on the chest
- ✔ coloration of underwing and underparts
- ✔ size of bill
- ✔ overall size of bird
- ✔ tail length
- ✔ call, especially mimicked part

Pin-tailed Whydah (female)

Yellow-mantled Widowbird (non-breeding male)

The calls of bishops and allied species are not unlike the 'swizzling' calls of weavers, but in many cases they are even more musical and in some instances more metallic. Indigobird calls play a crucial role in correctly identifying these species in all plumages. They comprise a series of rapid, jumbled sounds that include the mimicked calls of the indigobird's host species. The call excluding the mimicry varies significantly from one region to the next, and it is only the imitation of the host's call (both song and begging) that remains constant within a species. Comparative track 184 is helpful in not only indicating what to listen for, but in including excerpts of the hosts' calls.

BISHOPS & ALLIED SPECIES CAN BE DIVIDED INTO FOUR VISUAL GROUPS

Head broadly striped
(page 98)

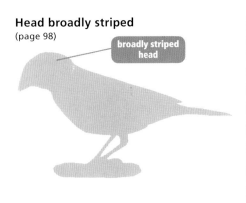

broadly striped head

Head not broadly striped, tail short, bill dull and symmetrical (page 103)

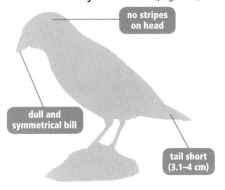

no stripes on head

dull and symmetrical bill

tail short (3.1–4 cm)

Head not broadly striped, tail short, bill or eye-ring diagnostic (page 102)

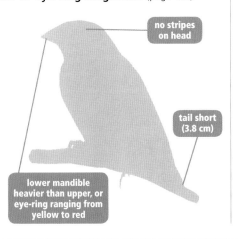

no stripes on head

tail short (3.8 cm)

lower mandible heavier than upper, or eye-ring ranging from yellow to red

Head not broadly striped, tail comparatively long (page 106)

no stripes on head

tail long (4.4–9.5 cm)

Pin-tailed Whydah
(female & non-breeding male)
Vidua macroura
Koningrooibekkie

dark pink to red bill

shortish tail

blue-grey legs

Length 12 cm (breeding male has 22-cm tail)
Weight 15 g
Habitat Open woodland, grassland, forest edges, croplands and gardens.
Habits Usually in small groups, the males obvious in the breeding season. Lays eggs mainly in Common Waxbill nests.

Call Nondescript chirping. The breeding male emits a high-pitched chirping that pulsates as he bobs in his display flight. Sounds fuller and more energetic than that of Red-collared Widowbird.
Comparative track 163

Shaft-tailed Whydah
(female & non-breeding male)
Vidua regia
Pylstertrooibekkie

pale rufous wash to head

stout pinkish bill

pinkish legs

Length 11 cm (breeding male has 24-cm tail)
Weight 15 g
Habitat Dry woodland, except broad-leaved.
Habits Solitary or in pairs. Lays eggs mainly in Violet-eared Waxbill nests.

Call Nondescript chirping. The breeding male emits a series of canary-like phrases but with more 'swizzling' and some piercing whistles. Also an agitated *chik*.

Long-tailed Paradise-Whydah
(female & non-breeding male)

Vidua paradisaea
Gewone Paradysvink

- striped head and face
- dark grey bill
- Visually inseparable from Broad-tailed Paradise-Whydah
- dark legs

Length 15 cm (breeding male has 29-cm tail)
Weight 20 g
Habitat Dry, open savanna and woodland.
Habits Usually in flocks. The breeding male is obvious when displaying. Lays eggs mainly in Green-winged Pytilia nests.

TRACK 109 **Call** Nondescript chirping. The breeding male emits a series of very high-pitched whistles, almost like those of a Spotted Flycatcher, coupled with cackling churring and swallow-like notes.

AT A GLANCE

✔ Dark grey bill
✔ Dark legs
✔ Striped head and face

 Similar-looking species Broad-tailed Paradise-Whydah, female and juvenile (page 99)

 Similar-sounding species None

NOTE Visually indistinguishable from the female and juvenile Broad-tailed Paradise-Whydah.

Broad-tailed Paradise-Whydah
(female & non-breeding male)

Vidua obtusa
Breëstertparadysvink

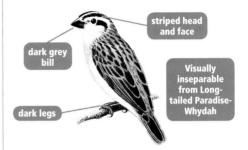

- striped head and face
- dark grey bill
- Visually inseparable from Long-tailed Paradise-Whydah
- dark legs

Length 15 cm (breeding male has 20-cm tail)
Weight 20 g
Habitat Broad-leaved woodland.
Habits Solitary or in pairs or small flocks. The breeding male is obvious when displaying. Lays eggs mainly in Orange-winged Pytilia nests.

Call Nondescript chirping. The breeding male emits a series of high-pitched sunbird-like whistles mixed with notes similar to those of Terrestrial Brownbul.

AT A GLANCE

✔ Dark grey bill
✔ Dark legs
✔ Striped head and face

 Similar-looking species Long-tailed Paradise-Whydah, female and juvenile (page 99)

 Similar-sounding species None

NOTE Visually indistinguishable from the female and juvenile Long-tailed Paradise-Whydah.

Dusky Indigobird
(female & non-breeding male)
Vidua funerea
Gewone Blouvinkie

white bill

pinkish to pale legs

Length 11 cm **Weight** 15 g
Habitat Woodland, riverine and montane forest, croplands and gardens.
Habits Solitary or in pairs. Lays eggs in African Firefinch nests.

Call Some non-breeding birds mimic the popping rattle of the African Firefinch, but are not nearly as vocal as in the breeding season, when the call is a range of chirps that includes mimicry of the African Firefinch.
Comparative track 172

AT A GLANCE

✔ White bill
✔ Pinkish to pale legs
✔ Call

 Similar-looking species Purple (page 100), Twinspot (page 101) and Village (northern Zimbabwe race) indigobirds, females and non-breeding males (page 101)

 Similar-sounding species Purple (track 111), Twinspot (track 112) and Village (track 113) indigobirds

NOTE Female Dusky and Purple indigobirds are considered inseparable in the field, but the non-breeding male Dusky Indigobird has very red legs. It resembles the pale-billed race of Village Indigobird in northern Zimbabwe, but their ranges do not overlap.

Purple Indigobird
(female & non-breeding male)
Vidua purpurascens
Witpootblouvinkie

white bill

pinkish to pale legs

Length 10 cm **Weight** 13 g
Habitat Dry woodland, riverine forest and croplands.
Habits Solitary or in pairs. Lays eggs in Jameson Firefinch nests.

Call Some non-breeding birds mimic the high-pitched bubbling warble of Jameson's Firefinch, but are not nearly as vocal as in the breeding season, when the call is a range of chirps that includes mimicry of Jameson's Firefinch.
Comparative track 172

AT A GLANCE

✔ White bill
✔ Pinkish to pale legs
✔ Call

 Similar-looking species Dusky (page 100), Twinspot (page 101) and Village (northern Zimbabwe race) indigobirds, females and non-breeding males (page 101)

 Similar-sounding species Dusky (track 110), Twinspot (track 112) and Village (track 113) indigobirds

NOTE Female Purple and Dusky indigobirds are considered inseparable in the field, but the non-breeding male Purple Indigobird has dull pink legs. It resembles the pale-billed race of Village Indigobird in northern Zimbabwe, which has more richly coloured legs.

Twinspot Indigobird
(female & non-breeding male)
Vidua codringtoni
Groenblouvinkie

white bill

greyish chest

reddish legs

Length 10 cm **Weight** 13 g
Habitat Riverine forest and dense bush.
Habits Solitary or in pairs or groups. Lays eggs in Red-throated Twinspot nests.

TRACK 112 **Call** Some non-breeding birds mimic the *tseep-tseep-tseep-trrrrrr* of Red-throated Twinspot, but are not nearly as vocal as in the breeding season, when the call is a range of chirps that includes mimicry of the Red-throated Twinspot.
Comparative track 172

AT A GLANCE

✔ White bill
✔ Reddish legs
✔ Greyish chest
✔ Call

 Similar-looking species Dusky (page 100), Purple (page 100) and Village (northern Zimbabwe race) indigobirds, females and non-breeding males (page 101)

 Similar-sounding species Dusky (track 110), Purple (track 111) and Village (track 113) indigobirds

NOTE The greyish chest is a useful identifying feature, but the call is still the best guide.

Village Indigobird
(female & non-breeding male)
Vidua chalybeata
Staalblouvinkie

dull buff wash to head

comparatively small pink to red bill

pinkish legs

Length 11 cm **Weight** 12 g
Habitat Acacia woodland near water and mopane woodland.
Habits Solitary or in pairs or groups; larger flocks in breeding season. Lays eggs in Red-billed Firefinch nests.

TRACK 113 **Call** Some non-breeding birds mimic the swallow-like calls of Red-billed Firefinch, but are not nearly as vocal as in the breeding season, when the call is a range of chirps that includes mimicry of the Red-billed Firefinch.
Comparative track 172

AT A GLANCE

✔ Comparatively small pink to red bill
✔ Pinkish legs
✔ Dull buff wash to head
✔ Call

 Similar-looking species Shaft-tailed Whydah, female and non-breeding male (page 98); Dusky (northern Zimbabwe race) (page 100), Purple (page 100) and Twinspot (page 101) indigobirds, females and non-breeding males

 Similar-sounding species Dusky (track 110), Purple (track 111) and Twinspot (track 112) indigobirds

NOTE The pale-billed race in northern Zimbabwe resembles Dusky, Purple and Twinspot indigobirds (its range does not overlap with that of Purple Indigobird). Bill size and head coloration are the best clues when separating female/non-breeding male Shaft-tailed Whydahs and Village Indigobirds.

Cuckoo Finch
(female & non-breeding male)
Anomalospiza imberbis
Koekoekvink

short, heavy bill with deeper lower mandible

Length 13 cm **Weight** 20 g
Habitat Open woodland and croplands.
Habits Solitary or in pairs. Lays eggs in a wide range of cisticola and prinia nests.

Call Nondescript chirps. The breeding male emits a soft, garbled mix of parrot-like notes.

AT A GLANCE
✔ Short, heavy bill with deeper lower mandible
✔ Call

Similar-looking species None (the heavy bill is distinctive)

Similar-sounding species None

Red-billed Quelea
(breeding female & non-breeding male)
Quelea quelea
Rooibekkwelea

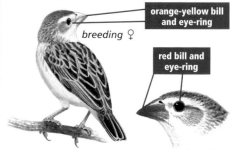

orange-yellow bill and eye-ring

breeding ♀

red bill and eye-ring

non-breeding
♂ and ♀

Length 12 cm **Weight** 20 g
Habitat Thornveld, grassland and croplands.
Habits In huge flocks, like moving clouds when in flight. Monogamous.

TRACK
114

Call Nondescript chirps. The breeding male emits weaver-like 'swizzling' sounds, like Cape Weaver, with additional soft whistles.
Comparative track 174

Female

AT A GLANCE
✔ Orange-yellow bill and eye-ring (breeding female)
✔ Red bill and eye-ring (non-breeding male and female)

Similar-looking species None (the eye-ring is distinctive)

Similar-sounding species Cape Weaver (track 104); Red-headed Quelea

NOTE The breeding male shows a large variation in facial patterning. The coloration of the breeding female's bill and eye-ring ranges from yellow to a deep orange.

Red-headed Quelea
(female & non-breeding male)
Quelea erythrops
Rooikopkwelea

Cardinal Quelea
(female & non-breeding male)
Quelea cardinalis
Kardinaalkwelea

bulky appearance

very short tail

comparatively long bill

slender appearance

comparatively short, stubby bill

very short tail

Length 11 cm; tail 3.3 cm **Weight** 20 g
Habitat Grassland and croplands, usually near water.
Habits In flocks of up to several hundred birds.

Call Nondescript chirps. The breeding male emits weaver-like 'swizzling' and twittering with nasal heavy breathing effect; no whistles.
Comparative track 174

Length 11 cm; tail 3.1 cm **Weight** 13 g
Habitat Tall or lightly wooded grassland.
Habits Occurs in flocks. Nomadic, following rainfall.

TRACK
115

Call Nondescript chirps. The breeding male emits accelerating weaver-like notes, ending in a nasal *meeeuuwww*.

Southern Red Bishop
(female & non-breeding male)
Euplectes orix
Rooivink

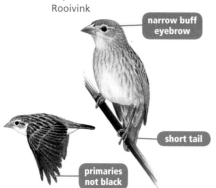

narrow buff eyebrow

short tail

primaries not black

Length 13 cm; tail 3.8 cm **Weight** 23 g
Habitat Open grassland, croplands and reed beds close to water.
Habits Occurs in flocks. Very territorial, the male's display flight characterised by very rapid wingbeats, like a bumblebee's.

TRACK 116 **Call** Nondescript chirps. The breeding male emits a 'swizzling' churring, with a distinctive *ti-teeeeeuuuu*.

Black-winged Bishop
(female & non-breeding male)
Euplectes hordeaceus
Vuurkopvink

heavy bill

short tail

primaries black

Length 12 cm; tail 4 cm **Weight** 22 g
Habitat Vegetation and grassland close to water, often in woodland.
Habits Usually occurs in small flocks. Forages mainly on the ground, but displays from a perch.

TRACK 117 **Call** Nondescript chirps. The breeding male emits a series of typical bishop 'swizzles' mixed with tseep notes and a distinctive *chi-chi-zweeee*.

AT A GLANCE
✔ Short tail
✔ Primaries not black
✔ Narrow buff eyebrow

 Similar-looking species Black-winged Bishop (page 104)

 Similar-sounding species None

NOTE Slightly longer tails separate the three bishops from the two queleas, which have very short tails.

AT A GLANCE
✔ Short tail
✔ Primaries black
✔ Heavy bill

 Similar-looking species Southern Red Bishop (page 104)

 Similar-sounding species None

NOTE Slightly longer tails separate the three bishops from the two queleas, which have very short tails.

Yellow-crowned Bishop
(female & non-breeding male)

Euplectes afer

Goudgeelvink

broad yellowish eyebrow

primaries not black

short tail

Length 11 cm; tail 3.7 cm **Weight** 15 g
Habitat Marshy reed beds in breeding season, but moves to drier areas when not breeding.
Habits Usually occurs in flocks.

TRACK 118

Call Nondescript chirps. The breeding male emits high-pitched tseeep notes and a distinctive nasal, insect-like churring. Softer and less metallic than that of Yellow Bishop.

Comparative track 173

AT A GLANCE

✔ Short tail
✔ Primaries not black
✔ Broad yellowish eyebrow

Similar-looking species None (combination of short tail and yellow eyebrow is distinctive)

Similar-sounding species Yellow Bishop (track 123)

NOTE Slightly longer tails separate the three bishops from the two queleas, which have very short tails.

Typical habitats for this visual group

Almost all of the bishops and their allied species can be found foraging and feeding in a range of grassland habitats.

Reed beds are the favoured breeding habitat for all the bishops.

Due to the abundance of food found in croplands, all the species in this group favour such areas.

White-winged Widowbird
(female & non-breeding male)
Euplectes albonotatus
Witvlerkflap

non-breeding ♂

pale underwing

small bill

comparatively narrow tail

yellow shoulder patch with white wing bar

♀

Length 15 cm; tail 4.5 cm (female), 5.3 cm (non-breeding male) **Weight** 20 g
Habitat Grassland and wetland.
Habits Often occurs in flocks when not breeding.

TRACK 119 Call Nondescript chirps. The breeding male emits a rustling sound, like a small animal in grass, and a metallic rattle very similar to that of River Warbler.
Comparative track 152

AT A GLANCE

FEMALE
✔ Comparatively narrow tail
✔ Pale underwing
✔ Small bill
NON-BREEDING MALE
✔ Yellow shoulder patch with white wing bar

Similar-looking species Long-tailed Widowbird (page 107); both have comparatively long tails, but the pale underwing in this species is distinctive

Similar-sounding species River Warbler (track 8)

Red-collared Widowbird
(female & non-breeding male)
Euplectes ardens
Rooikeelflap

non-breeding ♂

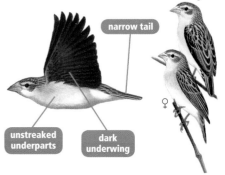

narrow tail

♀

unstreaked underparts

dark underwing

Length 12 cm; tail 4.4 cm (female), 5.5 cm (non-breeding male) **Weight** 20 g
Habitat Grassland, savanna and croplands.
Habits Usually occurs in flocks, associating with other seed-eaters when foraging on the ground.

TRACK 120 Call Nondescript chirps. The breeding male emits high-pitched *chip* notes and a metallic rattle, similar to that of Pin-tailed Whydah but thinner and higher-pitched.
Comparative track 163

AT A GLANCE

✔ Narrow tail
✔ Dark underwing
✔ Unstreaked underparts

Similar-looking species Yellow-mantled Widowbird (page 108), but the less bulky tail and smaller bill separate the species.

Similar-sounding species Pin-tailed Whydah (track 107)

Fan-tailed Widowbird
(female & non-breeding male)
Euplectes axillaris
Kortstertflap

red shoulder patch with no white wing bar

cinnamon under-wing, visible in flight (female)

♀

non-breeding ♂

Length 16 cm; tail 4.5 cm (female), 6.3 cm (non-breeding male) **Weight** 25 g
Habitat Grassland, reed beds and croplands.
Habits Usually occurs in flocks, associating with other seed-eaters.

TRACK 121 **Call** Nondescript chirps. The breeding male emits rhythmical, metallic and bubbly notes. **Comparative track** 173

AT A GLANCE

FEMALE
✔ Cinnamon underwing, visible in flight
NON-BREEDING MALE
✔ Red shoulder patch with no white wing bar

 Similar-looking species None

 Similar-sounding species Yellow-crowned Bishop (track 118)

NOTE Some females are cinnamon-coloured overall.

Long-tailed Widowbird
(female & non-breeding male)
Euplectes progne
Langstertflap

large size

bulky build

comparatively long, heavy, tapering tail

red shoulder patch with white bar below

non-breeding ♂

♀

Length 16 cm (female), 19 cm (non-breeding male); tail 6.2 cm (female), 9.5 cm (non-breeding male) **Weight** 30–40 g
Habitat Grassland and cropland, usually near water.
Habits Usually occurs in flocks.

TRACK 122 **Call** Nondescript chirps. The breeding male often emits a series of excited *chip-chip-chip-chip* and *churra-churra-churra* notes in display.

AT A GLANCE

FEMALE
✔ Comparatively long, heavy, tapering tail
✔ Large size
✔ Bulky build
NON-BREEDING MALE
✔ Red shoulder patch with white bar below

 Similar-looking species White-winged Widowbird (both have comparatively long tails)

 Similar-sounding species None

Yellow Bishop
(female & non-breeding male)
Euplectes capensis
Kaapse Flap

yellow rump

yellow shoulder and yellow rump

non-breeding ♂

♀

Length 15–18 cm; tail 5 cm **Weight** 35 g
Habitat Ranges from coastal fynbos and scrub to high-altitude grassland.
Habits Usually occurs in small family groups.

TRACK 123 **Call** Nondescript chirps. The breeding male emits a series of high-pitched *tseep* notes and a more energetic and metallic rattle than that of Yellow-crowned Bishop.
Comparative track 173

AT A GLANCE
FEMALE
✔ Yellow rump
NON-BREEDING MALE
✔ Yellow shoulder and yellow rump

Similar-looking species None (the yellow rump is distinctive)

Similar-sounding species Yellow-crowned Bishop (track 118)

Yellow-mantled Widowbird
(female & non-breeding male)
Euplectes macroura
Geelrugflap

♀

heavy bill

yellow shoulder patch with no white wing bar

bulky, non-tapering tail

dark underwing (female)

♀

buff rump

non-breeding ♂

Length 14 cm; tail 5.1 (female), 6.3 cm (non-breeding male) **Weight** 21 g
Habitat Wet grassland and reed beds.
Habits Sometimes occurs in flocks when not breeding.

Call Nondescript chirps. The breeding male emits rhythmical *ti-ti-cheeu* notes repeated several times at speed.

AT A GLANCE
FEMALE
✔ Bulky, non-tapering tail
✔ Heavy bill
✔ Dark underwing
NON-BREEDING MALE
✔ Bulky, non-tapering tail
✔ Buff rump
✔ Yellow shoulder patch with no white wing bar

Similar-looking species None (the bulky tail as well as buff underparts are distinctive)

Similar-sounding species None

Sparrows

The common House Sparrow is familiar to everyone and the sight of a small flock foraging on the ground and picking up seeds with its conical, typical seed-eater bill enables most people, birders or not, to recognise sparrows as a group (the exception is the Yellow-throated Petronia, which feeds in trees or on rocks and walks rather than hops). Confirmation is provided by the generally grey-brown plumage together with the rich rust coloration on the wings of most species. Bold head markings make the separation of male House, Cape and Great sparrows not too difficult, but identifying the females can be more challenging. The female House Sparrow has dark markings on the back that distinguish it from similarly coloured female bishops, while the broad white eyebrow, pale coloration and small bill of the petronia should help to separate it from similar-looking seed-eaters.

LOOK FOR

✔ **rump coloration**
✔ **head markings**
✔ **wing bars**
✔ **throat coloration**

House Sparrow (male and female)

Great Sparrow

SPARROWS CAN BE DIVIDED INTO TWO VISUAL GROUPS

Head with markings (page 110)

head markings, notably eyebrow

Head plain grey (page 112)

uniform grey head and face

House Sparrow
Passer domesticus
Huismossie

grey rump

buff back, streaked

buff eyebrow

buff rump

Length 15 cm **Weight** 25 g
Habitat Very common around human settlements.
Habits In pairs or small flocks.

TRACK 124 **Call** A typical sparrow *chir-ip* note, but more piercing than that of other sparrows. Also a jumble of *chir-ip* and *zeeu* sounds. The male gives a characteristic *de-zip* territorial call; the female may join in with an agitated chattering. The group contact call is a ratchety rattle.
Comparative track 175

AT A GLANCE

MALE
✔ Grey rump
FEMALE
✔ Buff rump
✔ Buff eyebrow
✔ Buff back, streaked

 Similar-looking species Great Sparrow (page 110) resembles the male, but check the rump colour; Yellow-throated Petronia (page 111) resembles the female

 Similar-sounding species Cape Sparrow (track 126)

Great Sparrow
Passer motitensis
Grootmossie

dull chestnut eyebrow

short white eyebrow reaching to bill

chestnut back, streaked

chestnut side of neck forms 'C' around face

chestnut rump

Length 16 cm **Weight** 32 g
Habitat Acacia woodland. Often found close to water in dry areas.
Habits Solitary or in pairs.

TRACK 125 **Call** Slow, drawn-out *chreeuu* notes and agitated chirps.
Comparative track 175

AT A GLANCE

MALE
✔ Chestnut rump
✔ Chestnut side of neck forms 'C' around face
✔ Chestnut back, streaked
✔ **Short white eyebrow reaching to bill**
FEMALE
✔ Chestnut rump
✔ Dull chestnut eyebrow
✔ Chestnut back, streaked

 Similar-looking species None (the chestnut 'C' around the face is distinctive, and the male's chestnut rump separates it from the male House Sparrow)

 Similar-sounding species Lesser (track 3) and Pallid (track 4) honeyguides; Cape (track 126), Southern Grey-headed (track 128) and Northern Grey-headed (track 129) sparrows

Cape Sparrow (female)
Passer melanurus
Gewone Mossie

- broken white 'C' around face
- plain back
- chestnut rump

Length 15 cm **Weight** 29 g
Habitat Varied, from dry areas to woodland, plantations, croplands and human settlements.
Habits Occurs in pairs or flocks, which are sometimes very large. Forages mainly on the ground, but also hawks insects.

TRACK 126 **Call** At dawn, chirps and similar notes, as *chree-cheeu-chip-cheep*. When in flocks, a series of rattles combined with *cheeu* notes. A group contact call is a short, liquid *churrr-rrr*.
Comparative track 175

Yellow-throated Petronia
Petronia superciliaris
Geelvlekmossie

- broad white eyebrow
- bill with horn-coloured upper mandible, pinkish lower mandible
- buff back, streaked

- yellow spot on throat (not often visible)

Length 15 cm **Weight** 24 g
Habitat Savanna woodland.
Habits Solitary or in pairs or flocks, moving about restlessly.

TRACK 127 **Call** Three or four *chirp-chirp-chirp* notes, with distinctive tone and sequence.

AT A GLANCE

✔ Plain back
✔ Chestnut rump
✔ Broken white 'C' around face

 Similar-looking species None (the broken white 'C' around the face is distinctive)

 Similar-sounding species Lesser (track 3) and Pallid (track 4) honeyguides; Great (track 125), Southern Grey-headed (track 128) and Northern Grey-headed (track 129) sparrows

AT A GLANCE

✔ Broad white eyebrow
✔ Buff back, streaked
✔ Bill with horn-coloured upper mandible, pinkish lower mandible
✔ Yellow spot on throat (not often visible)
✔ Call

 Similar-looking species House Sparrow, female (page 110)

 Similar-sounding species African Pipit (track 131)

NOTE The yellow spot on the throat is often hidden.

Southern Grey-headed Sparrow
Passer diffusus
Gryskopmossie

- compact bill, black in summer and horn-coloured in winter
- obvious white wing bar
- greyish throat

winter bill

Length 15 cm **Weight** 24 g
Habitat Woodland.
Habits Solitary or in pairs. Forages on ground.

 Call A series of *cheeuu* notes given in sequence and with very little variation. Agitated chirps when competing for food.
TRACK 128
Comparative track 175

AT A GLANCE

✔ Compact bill, black in summer & horn-coloured in winter
✔ Greyish throat
✔ Obvious white wing bar

Similar-looking species Northern Grey-headed Sparrow (page 112)

Similar-sounding species Lesser (track 3) and Pallid (track 4) honeyguides; Great (track 125), Cape (track 126) and Northern Grey-headed (track 129) sparrows

NOTE The head is less richly blue-grey than that of Northern Grey-headed Sparrow.

Northern Grey-headed Sparrow
Passer griseus
Witkeelmossie

- white wing bar inconspicuous or absent
- heavy bill, black all year
- white throat

Length 16 cm **Weight** 39 g
Habitat Woodland.
Habits Solitary or in pairs.

 Call A series of *cheeuu* notes given in sequence and with very little variation. Agitated chirps when competing for food.
TRACK 129
Comparative track 175

AT A GLANCE

✔ Heavy bill, black all year
✔ White throat
✔ White wing bar inconspicuous or absent

Similar-looking species Southern Grey-headed Sparrow (page 112)

Similar-sounding species Lesser (track 3) and Pallid (track 4) honeyguides; Great (track 125), Cape (track 126) and Southern Grey-headed (track 128) sparrows

NOTE The head is darker blue-grey than that of Southern Grey-headed Sparrow.

SEPARATING VISUAL GROUPS

STEP TWO

Pipits & longclaws

Being mainly ground-based, pipits are often confused with larks, but there are certain differences between the two groups. Like larks, pipits are small to medium-sized birds, but all species have slender, pointed bills. Pipits are less brightly coloured and less distinctively marked than larks, and they have longer, more slender legs that give them a characteristic gait. The fast pace at which they walk and dart about chasing insects is in stark contrast to larks' slower and more methodical search for seeds. Most pipits can be observed 'tail-wagging', which also helps to separate them from larks.

Pipits are nomadic, so distribution is a less important criterion for identification, especially in winter, when they tend to move around more; in summer, their whereabouts are generally more predictable. Calls can be helpful when separating some species, but for the most part pipits can be identified without paying much attention to their vocalisations. However – and especially if you are just beginning to familiarise yourself with the different pipits – it is useful to identify a bird first on its display call and then to observe how it behaves so that the next time you see it, you will recognise the species from its behaviour.

More important than vocalisations is pipits' habit of tail-wagging, although care should be exercised when the individuals are juvenile. Tail-wagging develops as the birds age, so the action of a youngster can be quite different from that of an adult bird of the same species. In general, juveniles are difficult to separate unless they are seen with adults. Also bear in mind that behavioural characteristics such as tail-wagging are best viewed once the birds have settled and are no longer stressed by your presence. If you are uncertain about an identification, watch the mystery bird for 10–15 minutes and you will get a better idea of its 'normal' behaviour.

Longclaws are closely related to pipits and have a similar build, but adults are easily distinguished by their richly coloured throats with contrasting black markings. Immature birds, however, are more drab in appearance and can be confused with adult pipits.

Long-billed Pipit

 LOOK FOR

✔ **tail-wagging and other behaviour**
✔ **back and chest markings**
✔ **rump markings**
✔ **tail length and/or length of wing in relation to tail**

Back streaked or scalloped, flanks not streaked (page 115)

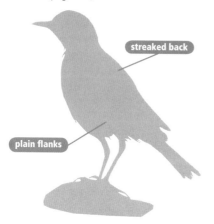

streaked back

plain flanks

Back and flanks streaked (page 121)

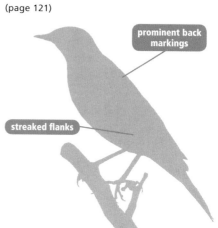

prominent back markings

streaked flanks

Back plain (page 119)

unmarked back

Plain-backed Pipit

Cape Longclaw (juvenile)
Macronyx capensis
Oranjekeeldalkoentjie

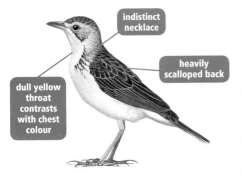

indistinct necklace

heavily scalloped back

dull yellow throat contrasts with chest colour

Length 20 cm; tail 6.6 cm **Weight** 46 g
Habitat Mostly open grasslands ranging from wet to high-altitude.
Habits Usually in pairs. Uses low perches. Often gives a cat-like meow when in flight.

TRACK
130

Call An unmistakable cat-like *meeeuuuwww*. Adult males emit an excited sparrow-like chirping when defending a territory. Birds also produce mournful single whistles about a second apart.

Wood Pipit
Anthus nyassae
Boskoester

shorter tail

runs along branches

Length 18 cm; tail 6.5 cm **Weight** 24 g
Habitat Short grass in woodland.
Habits Solitary or in pairs. Usually on the ground, but flies to a perch in a tree when disturbed, sometimes running along a branch.

Call In display, a repeated five-note sequence: *deeweet-cheoa-prrrree-tzoeu-prrrreuu*.
Comparative track 176

African Pipit
Anthus cinnamomeus
Gewone Koester

Mountain Pipit
Anthus hoeschi
Bergkoester

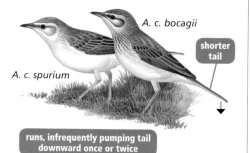

A. c. bocagii

shorter tail

A. c. spurium

shortish tail

runs, infrequently pumping tail downward once or twice

Length 16 cm; **tail** 6.2 cm **Weight** 27 g
Habitat Grassland and savanna, usually near water, preferring short grass and burned areas; below 2 000 m.
Habits Solitary or in pairs when breeding; often in groups when not breeding. Runs in bursts, occasionally pumping its tail downward once or twice at the end of a run; sometimes struts 'proudly'.

 TRACK 131 **Call** In display, a sequence of *chit-chit* notes starting with two and adding another at the end of each phrase, with a long flourish at the end.
Comparative track 177

Length 18 cm; **tail** 6.6 cm **Weight** 27 g
Habitat Montane grassland above 2 000 m.
Habits Solitary or in pairs or small groups. Usually on the ground, but sometimes seen on elevated perches.

 TRACK 132 **Call** In aerial display, a series of widely spaced, single *chirit* notes with a flurry at the end.
Similar to that of African Pipit, but a series of widely spaced notes rather than an increasing sequence.
Comparative track 177

AT A GLANCE

✔ Runs, infrequently pumping tail downward once or twice
✔ Shorter tail
✔ Habitat
✔ Display call

 Similar-looking species Mountain (page 116) and Kimberley (page 117) pipits

 Similar-sounding species Mountain Pipit (track 132)

NOTE African and Mountain pipits may overlap at lower altitudes, where call is an important aid in separating them. Kimberley Pipit may also be confused with African Pipit but has a longer tail.

AT A GLANCE

✔ Shortish tail
✔ Habitat
✔ Display call

 Similar-looking species African (page 116) and Kimberley (page 117) pipits

 Similar-sounding species African Pipit (track 131)

NOTE African and Mountain pipits may overlap at lower altitudes, where call is an important aid in separating them. Very little is known about Mountain Pipit behaviour.

Kimberley Pipit
Anthus pseudosimilis
Kimberleykoester

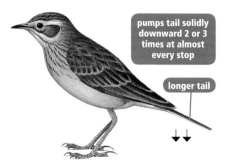

pumps tail solidly downward 2 or 3 times at almost every stop

longer tail

Length 18 cm; tail 6.5 cm (female), 9 cm (male) **Weight** 32 g
Habitat Short, sparse vegetation where there are no stones or rocks; below 2 000 m.
Habits Solitary or in pairs. Usually on the ground, but flies to a perch when disturbed. As it walks, pumps tail solidly downward two or three times at almost every stop. Its gait is more of a stroll than the strut of African Pipit.

TRACK 133 **Call** Mainly a repeated three-note *tzeeu-pree-cheeu*, each note at a lower pitch than the previous one; also a two-note *zee-zeeu*.
Comparative track 176

AT A GLANCE

✔ Longer tail
✔ Pumps tail solidly downward 2 or 3 times at almost every stop
✔ Habitat
✔ Display call

Similar-looking species African page 116) and Mountain (page 116) pipits

Similar-sounding species Long-billed (track 134), Wood, Plain-backed (track 137) and Buffy pipits

NOTE The male Kimberley Pipit has the longest tail of any pipit in the region, whereas the tail of the female is comparative in length to that of other pipits. A pair of Kimberley Pipits seen together is therefore easily recognised.

Long-billed Pipit
Anthus similis
Nicholsonse Koester

weak and infrequent tail flicking

longer tail

Length 18 cm; tail 7 cm **Weight** 30 g
Habitat Rock-strewn slopes in dry and grassy areas; also woodland.
Habits Mostly solitary or in pairs, but occasionally also in small flocks. Usually on the ground, but sometimes uses an elevated perch. Flicks tail weakly and infrequently.

TRACK 134 **Call** A series of single-noted, sparrow-like chirps, descending in pitch; less monotonous than that of Kimberley Pipit.
Comparative track 176

AT A GLANCE

✔ Longer tail
✔ Weak and infrequent tail flicking
✔ Habitat

Similar-looking species Kimberley (page 117) and Wood (page 115) pipits

Similar-sounding species Kimberley (track 133), Wood, Plain-backed (track 137) and Buffy pipits

NOTE The indistinctly streaked back makes this species a candidate for either the streaked back or the plain back group. Like Wood Pipit, it may flush into a tree, but its different markings and longer tail help to separate it from that species. Care should also be taken when separating Long-billed and Kimberley pipits: the much longer tail of the male Kimberley Pipit should be helpful.

Yellow-breasted Pipit
(female & non-breeding male)
Anthus chloris
Geelborskoester

colour of throat and chest the same

heavily scalloped back

indistinctly streaked breast band

yellow belly spot (not always visible)

Length 17 cm; tail 6.6 cm **Weight** 25 g
Habitat Montane grassland, usually on flatter slopes.
Habits Solitary or in pairs, but sometimes also in small flocks. Stays low and will run rather than fly away when disturbed.

TRACK **135** **Call** An excited rattle, similar to the sound of a playing card hitting the spokes of a bicycle wheel. Also *cheeu* (like that of a Scarlet-chested Sunbird) or sometimes *too-ee* (like that of a Willow Warbler).

AT A GLANCE
✔ Heavily scalloped back
✔ Indistinctly streaked breast band
✔ Colour of throat and chest the same
✔ Yellow belly spot (not always visible)
✔ Call

Similar-looking species None (the yellow belly spot is distinctive)

Similar-sounding species None

Golden Pipit (female)
Tmetothylacus tenellus
Goudkoester

no streaking on chest

unfeathered tibia

yellowish wash overall

Length 15 cm; tail 6 cm **Weight** 20 g
Habitat Dry grassland.
Habits Solitary in the region. Perches in trees or on bushes.

TRACK **136** **Call** A distinctive rhythmical series of sunbird-like chirps, *chit-chit-chiree-chiroo-chit*, sometimes with additional notes at the end. The call is very soft and birds are more likely to be seen before they are heard.

AT A GLANCE
✔ Unfeathered tibia
✔ No streaking on chest
✔ Yellowish wash overall

Similar-looking species None (the lack of feathers on the tibia is distinctive)

Similar-sounding species None

NOTE A rare vagrant, mostly November to February.

Plain-backed Pipit
Anthus leucophrys
Donkerkoester

Buffy Pipit
Anthus vaalensis
Vaalkoester

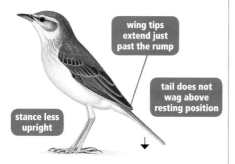

wing tips extend just past the rump

tail does not wag above resting position

stance less upright

wing tips extend just past the rump

stance very upright

tail wags above and below resting position

Length 17 cm; tail 6.5 cm **Weight** 27 g
Habitat Sandy and burned areas in very short grassland.
Habits Usually solitary or in pairs, but sometimes in small flocks. Walks upright, but its stance is less upright than that of Buffy Pipit. Tail wagging takes the form of repeated strong downward pumping, the tail not rising above the resting position.

 TRACK 137 **Call** Mostly a three-noted *zeea-treeu-preeu*, the second note lower than the first and the last note slightly higher than the second; less frequently, a two-noted *zee-zeeoot*.
Comparative track 176

Length 18 cm; tail 7.3 cm **Weight** 29 g
Habitat Sandy and burned areas in short grassland.
Habits Usually solitary or in pairs, but sometimes in small flocks. Takes a short run, stops and stands very upright. Raises head from time to time while foraging. Wags tail slowly and deliberately, raising it above and below the resting position.

Call A very fast *pree-ree-oo* and a jumble of sparrow-like *treeuu*, *chree* and *preeu* notes with no definite pattern. The alarm call is more like that of a wagtail than of a sparrow.
Comparative track 176

Long-tailed Pipit
Anthus longicaudatus
Langstertkoester

wing tips extend to a third or half the length of the tail

stance very slouched

tail wags above and below resting position almost continuously

Length 18 cm; tail 7.8 cm **Weight** 31 g
Habitat Short grassland and open areas.
Habits Either solitary or in large flocks of more than 30. Forages horizontally, like a wagtail. Wags tail deliberately, raising it above and below the resting position.

Call Typical pipit flight and alarm calls. Breeding display call not yet described.

AT A GLANCE

✔ Wing tips extend to a third or half the length of the tail
✔ Stance very slouched
✔ Tail wags above and below resting position almost continuously

 Similar-looking species Plain-backed (page 119) and Buffy (page 119) pipits

 Similar-sounding species None

NOTE A non-breeding winter visitor with a restricted range in South Africa. Tail wagging is similar to that of Buffy Pipit, but this species' long wing projection almost halfway along the tail gives it a long and slender appearance. It also has a proportionately smaller head and bill than Buffy Pipit.

African Rock Pipit
Anthus crenatus
Klipkoester

uniform dark bill

wing tips extend just past the rump

no tail wagging

Length 18 cm; tail 6.2 cm **Weight** 30 g
Habitat Rocky outcrops above 1 000 m.
Habits Either solitary or in pairs. Usually seen as it forages on the ground.

 TRACK **138** **Call** A descending shrill whistle followed by a single- or double-noted trill, like a sound effect in an electronic game.

AT A GLANCE

✔ Wing tips extend just past the rump
✔ Uniform dark bill
✔ No tail wagging
✔ Call

 Similar-looking species None (the uniform dark bill is distinctive)

 Similar-sounding species None

Short-tailed Pipit
Anthus brachyurus
Kortstertkoester

mottled, dark back

bold streaking on chest

smaller than sparrow

Length 12 cm **Weight** 16 g
Habitat Short grassland in hilly areas.
Habits Usually solitary or in pairs. Very rarely uses elevated perches.

Call Soft, liquid nasal notes, similar to that of Rudd's Lark.

AT A GLANCE
✔ Mottled, dark back
✔ Bold streaking on chest
✔ Smaller than sparrow

Similar-looking species Bushveld Pipit (page 121)

Similar-sounding species Rudd's Lark (track 55)

NOTE Can be confused with a non-breeding bishop. A 'bishop' with white outertail feathers should be examined more closely.

Bushveld Pipit
Anthus caffer
Bosveldkoester

light-coloured back

smaller than sparrow

streaking on chest less prominent

Length 13 cm **Weight** 17 g
Habitat Open broad-leaved and savanna woodland, and burned areas.
Habits Solitary or in pairs. Usually remains on the ground.

TRACK 139

Call A nasal *zeee-ip, zeee-oo* that continues rhythmically, and a series of descending nasal notes similar to that of Lesser Striped Swallow but more piercing and without a distinctive rhythm. Also a piercing *dzeep* alarm or flight call.

AT A GLANCE
✔ Light-coloured back
✔ Streaking on chest less prominent
✔ Smaller than sparrow
✔ Call

Similar-looking species Short-tailed Pipit (page 121)

Similar-sounding species None

NOTE The streaking on the flanks can be minimal and may be obscured by the folded wing, sometimes making the flanks appear plain. Careful observation should be made with any heavily streaked pipit with plain flanks.

Striped Pipit
Anthus lineiventris
Gestreepte Koester

yellow edges to wing feathers

belly and flanks streaked

rump not streaked

Length 18 cm **Weight** 34 g
Habitat Rocky areas with broad-leaved woodland.
Habits Usually seen singing from a prominent perch in a tree. Forages among rocks.

TRACK **140** **Call** Bold and very musical chirps, similar to that of African Pied Wagtail, although phrasing is very variable. Less thrush-like than that of Tree Pipit.

AT A GLANCE

✔ Rump not streaked
✔ Belly and flanks streaked
✔ Yellow edges to wing feathers
✔ Call

 Similar-looking species None (the streaking on the belly and flanks is distinctive)

 Similar-sounding species None

Tree Pipit
Anthus trivialis
Boomkoester

rump not streaked

belly not streaked

same size as a sparrow

Length 14 cm **Weight** 22 g
Habitat Open grassland with large trees.
Habits Solitary or in pairs or small flocks. Flies up into a tree when disturbed.

 TRACK **141** **Call** Only flight and contact calls are heard in southern Africa. Elsewhere, melodic with canary-like phrases, like that of Karoo Thrush. Call not as wagtail-like as that of Striped Pipit.

AT A GLANCE

✔ Rump not streaked
✔ Belly not streaked
✔ Same size as a sparrow
✔ Call

 Similar-looking species None (the unstreaked belly is distinctive)

 Similar-sounding species None

NOTE A summer migrant (October to April).

Red-throated Pipit
(non-breeding) *Anthus cervinus*
Rooikeelkoester

streaked rump

same size as
a sparrow

belly not
streaked

Length 14 cm **Weight** 20 g
Habitat Short grassland near water.
Habits Probably solitary in the region.

TRACK
142

Call Probably silent in southern
Africa. Elsewhere, a very musical,
canary-like song comprising various
warbles, and a single piercing *dzee* note similar
to the single-note call of Cape White-eye, but
shorter and harsher.

AT A GLANCE

✔ Streaked rump
✔ Belly not streaked
✔ Same size as a sparrow
✔ Call

 Similar-looking species None (the
streaked rump is distinctive)

 Similar-sounding species None

NOTE A rare vagrant.

Typical habitats for this visual group

*Short grassland, often near water, is an ideal
habitat for both the Short-tailed and the rare
Red-throated Pipit.*

*The Bushveld Pipit is found in grassland with
large trees. Although this habitat is shared
by the Tree Pipit, the latter is a less common
summer visitor and, due to its hill-topping
behaviour, favours clumps of woodland at
the tops of hilly areas.*

Canaries & allied species

Canaries, seedeaters and siskins make up a large group of seed-eating birds that are recognised by their stout, conical bills. They are generally smaller than sparrows and weavers, and whereas the males are often quite brightly coloured, the females tend to be brown or grey. Apart from the size difference, female canaries and their allies can be distinguished from sparrows in that they lack the latter's combination of warm brown coloration and distinctive plumage patterns.

Also unlike sparrows, which pick up seeds only on the ground, canaries forage on grasses and shrubs too. Their calls are very melodic, comprising bubbly, liquid and tuneful notes.

LOOK FOR

✔ rump coloration
✔ head, face, throat and chest markings
✔ the extent of yellow in the plumage
✔ tips to wings and/or tail

Black-throated Canary (female)

Black-throated Canary (male)

CANARIES & ALLIED SPECIES CAN BE DIVIDED INTO FOUR VISUAL GROUPS

Grey or pale brown overall, with a yellow rump (page 126)

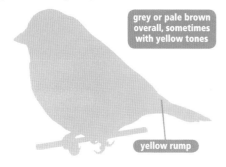

grey or pale brown overall, sometimes with yellow tones

yellow rump

Chestnut or cinnamon overall (page 130)

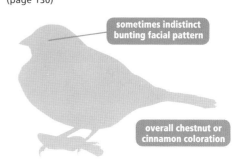

sometimes indistinct bunting facial pattern

overall chestnut or cinnamon coloration

Grey overall, with a grey or brown rump (page 128)

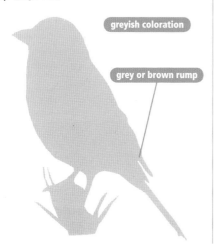

greyish coloration

grey or brown rump

Drab yellow, with plain upperparts (page 131)

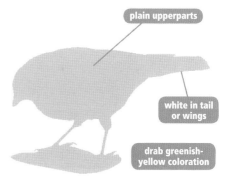

plain upperparts

white in tail or wings

drab greenish-yellow coloration

Black-throated Canary
Crithagra atrogularis
Bergkanarie

grey-brown throat

uniform yellow rump

small black throat patch

♂

pale tips to tail

♀

yellow rump and white uppertail coverts

Length 11 cm **Weight** 13 g
Habitat Woodland, grassland and croplands.
Habits In pairs or flocks. Forages on the ground or in trees.

 TRACK 143 **Call** An energetic series of typical canary notes, with distinctive Cape Sparrow notes and piercing whistles in the phrasing.
Comparative track 178

Male

AT A GLANCE

MALE
✔ Uniform yellow rump
✔ Pale tips to tail
✔ Small black throat patch
FEMALE
✔ Yellow rump and white uppertail coverts
✔ Pale tips to tail
✔ Grey-brown throat

 Similar-looking species None

Similar-sounding species White-throated Canary (track 145)

Lemon-breasted Canary
(female) *Crithagra citrinipectus*
Geelborskanarie

rump and tail coverts uniform yellow

pale buffy throat

pale tips to tail

Length 12 cm **Weight** 11 g
Habitat Woodland, grassland and savanna.
Habits In pairs or flocks. Forages on the ground or in trees.

Call Short bursts of jumbled, typical canary or warbler-like phrases, with a pause between each phrase.
Comparative track 178

Male (left), female (right)

AT A GLANCE

✔ Pale tips to tail
✔ Rump and tail coverts uniform yellow
✔ Pale buffy throat

 Similar-looking species None

 Similar-sounding species None

NOTE The pale tips to the tail may be difficult to see if the plumage is worn.

Yellow Canary (female)
Crithagra flaviventris
Geelkanarie

rump and upper tail coverts greenish yellow

underparts variably streaked

plain browish tail with yellow edging to feathers

Length 14 cm **Weight** 18 g
Habitat Open shrubland at a range of altitudes.
Habits Usually in flocks, often with other canaries. Forages on the ground.

TRACK **144**

Call A series of typical canary notes without pause; a single phrase can last for up to 20 seconds.
Comparative track 178

White-throated Canary
Crithagra albogularis
Witkeelkanarie

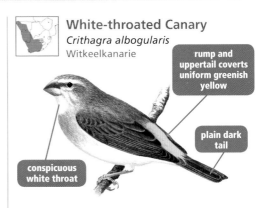

rump and uppertail coverts uniform greenish yellow

plain dark tail

conspicuous white throat

Length 15 cm **Weight** 27 g
Habitat Shrubland, sometimes on rocky slopes.
Habits Usually in pairs or small flocks. Forages on the ground.

TRACK **145**

Call A series of short, typical canary notes with long pauses between phrases. The song is full and liquid, often ending in a Bokmakierie-like *puurrr*.
Comparative track 178

Black-eared Seedeater
Crithagra mennelli
Swartoorkanarie

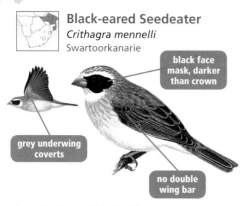

black face mask, darker than crown

grey underwing coverts

no double wing bar

Length 13 cm **Weight** 15 g
Habitat Woodland associated with Kalahari sand.
Habits Solitary or in pairs or small flocks. Forages on the ground and among bushes.

TRACK **146** **Call** Similar basic notes to those of Streaky-headed Seedeater but with jumbled phrases like those of Cape White-eye.
Comparative track 178

AT A GLANCE

✔ No double wing bar
✔ Black face mask, darker than crown
✔ Grey underwing coverts
✔ Call

Similar-looking species Dark-cheeked race of Streaky-headed Seedeater (page 128)

Similar-sounding species None

NOTE Streaking on the chest of this species and Streaky-headed Seedeater is variable and not a reliable feature; the colour of the underwing coverts is most reliable for separating these species.

Streaky-headed Seedeater
Crithagra gularis
Streepkopkanarie

no double wing bar

buff underwing coverts

cheeks same colour as crown

Length 15 cm **Weight** 20 g
Habitat Various woodland types, in rocky hills and open areas; also forest edges.
Habits Usually in pairs or small flocks. Forages on the ground and in trees; easily missed.

TRACK **147** **Call** A wide range of musical notes, including a distinctive, almost parrot-like *si-ree* or *si-ree-oo*.
Comparative track 178

AT A GLANCE

✔ No double wing bar
✔ Buff underwing coverts
✔ Cheeks same colour as crown
✔ Call

Similar-looking species The dark-cheeked race resembles Black-eared Seedeater (page 128)

Similar-sounding species None

NOTE Streaking on the chest of this species and Black-eared Seedeater is variable and not a reliable feature; the colour of the underwing coverts is most reliable for separating these species. *Humilis* race is darker overall but cheeks always match crown.

Protea Seedeater
Crithagra leucoptera
Witvlerkkanarie

double white wing bar

Typical habitats for this visual group

Fynbos and protea stands are home to the range-bound Protea Seedeater.

Forest edges also provide suitable habitat for Protea and Streaky-headed seedeaters.

Length 15 cm **Weight** 22 g
Habitat Fynbos, especially protea stands; also dense bush and forest edges.
Habits Solitary or in pairs or small groups. Forages in the canopy of trees and bushes, where it is easily missed.

TRACK 148 **Call** A typical canary introductory phrase followed by an agitated series of repeated *chur-chur-chur...tirup-tirup-tirup* notes.
Comparative track 178

AT A GLANCE

✔ **Double white wing bar**
✔ **Call**

 Similar-looking species None (the double wing bar is distinctive)

 Similar-sounding species None

Black-headed Canary
(female) *Serinus alario*
Swartkopkanarie

uniform grey head and chest

chestnut wing

chestnut tail

Length 13 cm **Weight** 12 g
Habitat Arid and semi-arid shrubland.
Habits In pairs or small flocks in breeding season; large flocks when not breeding. Forages in bushes and on the ground.

TRACK 149

Call The most warbler-like of all canary calls, but with weaver-like 'swizzling' and rising nasal whistles.
Comparative track 178

Lark-like Bunting
Emberiza impetuani
Vaalstreepkoppie

indistinct buff malar stripe and eyebrow

overall cinnamon wash

rufous edge to wing feathers

Length 14 cm **Weight** 15 g
Habitat Very short grassland, shrublands and rocky outcrops in dry areas.
Habits Usually in small groups, but sometimes in large flocks. Associates with sparrowlarks. Forages on the ground.

TRACK 150

Call Thrush-like, with a weaver's 'swizzle', often repeated.
Comparative track 178

AT A GLANCE
✔ Uniform grey head and chest
✔ Chestnut wing
✔ Chestnut tail

Similar-looking species None

Similar-sounding species None

AT A GLANCE
✔ Overall cinnamon wash
✔ Indistinct buff malar stripe and eyebrow
✔ Rufous edge to wing feathers
✔ Call

Similar-looking species None

Similar-sounding species None

Cape Siskin
Crithagra totta
Kaapse Pietjiekanarie

Drakensberg Siskin
Crithagra symonsi
Bergpietjiekanarie

white tips to primaries

white tips to tail

white outer-tail feathers

Length 13 cm **Weight** 11 g
Habitat Montane grassland and shrublands.
Habits In pairs or flocks. Forages among rocks and grass tufts.

Call Very musical and almost identical to a caged canary, with distinctive canary whistles.
Comparative track 178

Length 12 cm **Weight** 11 g
Habitat Montane forest patches and fynbos; also edges of plantations.
Habits Usually in pairs or small flocks, but larger groups also occur. Forages on the ground or on vegetation.

TRACK 151 **Call** Almost warbler-like, comprising a series of rising and falling whistles and swizzles.
Comparative track 178

AT A GLANCE

✔ White tips to primaries
✔ White tips to tail
✔ Distribution
✔ Call

 Similar-looking species None (the white-tipped primaries are distinctive)

 Similar-sounding species None

NOTE The white tips to the primaries are not always visible on the female, but the different distributions of Cape and Drakensberg siskins make identification easy.

AT A GLANCE

✔ White outertail feathers
✔ Distribution
✔ Call

 Similar-looking species None (the white outertail feathers are distinctive)

 Similar-sounding species None

NOTE The white outertail feathers are not always visible, but the different distributions of Drakensberg and Cape siskins make identification easy.

appendix

In order that similar-looking species could be grouped together for comparative purposes, strict taxonomic sequences have not been adhered to in the 'family' groups described in this book. For those interested in taxonomic relationships, the groupings in this book are represented by the following families and genera. Note that, taxonomically, warblers comprise a large group that includes cisticolas and prinias (Cisticolidae) as well as 'true' warblers (Sylviidae).

Honeyguides & honeybirds
Family: Indicatoridae
Genera: *Indicator* (Greater, Lesser, Pallid and Scaly-throated honeyguides); *Prodotiscus* (Brown-backed and Green-backed honeybirds).

True warblers & allied species
Family: Sylviidae
Genera: *Acrocephalus* (Sedge and Marsh warblers, Greater and Lesser swamp-warblers, and Basra, African, Eurasian and Great reed-warblers); *Sylvia* (Common Whitethroat, Garden Warbler); *Luscinia* (Thrush Nightingale); *Locustella* (River Warbler); *Schoenicola* (Broad-tailed Warbler); *Hippolais* (Olive-tree and Icterine warblers); *Bradypterus* (Barratt's and Knysna warblers, and Little Rush-Warbler); *Phylloscopus* (Willow Warbler).

Cisticolas
Family: Cisticolidae
Genera: *Cisticola* (Zitting, Desert, Cloud, Wing-snapping, Pale-crowned, Croaking, Short-winged, Singing, Lazy, Red-faced, Chirping, Rufous-winged, Luapula, Levaillant's, Grey-backed, Tinkling, Wailing and Rattling cisticolas, and Neddicky); *Heliolais* (Red-winged Warbler).

Prinias & prinia-like warblers
Family: Cisticolidae
Genera: *Prinia* (Tawny-flanked, Black-chested, Drakensberg and Karoo prinias); *Oreophilais* (Roberts's Warbler); *Phragmacia* (Namaqua Warbler).

Larks & sparrowlarks
Family: Alaudidae
Genera: *Eremopterix* (Black-eared, Chestnut-backed and Grey-backed sparrowlarks); *Heteromirafra* (Rudd's Lark); *Spizocorys* (Botha's, Stark's, Pink-billed and Sclater's larks); *Ammomanopsis* (Gray's Lark); *Certhilauda* (Cape, Agulhas, Karoo, Benguela and Eastern long-billed larks, and Short-clawed Lark); *Chersomanes* (Spike-heeled Lark); *Mirafra* (Eastern and Cape clapper larks, and Monotonous, Flappet, Melodious and Rufous-naped larks); *Calendulauda* (Fawn-coloured, Karoo, Barlow's, Red, Dune and Sabota larks); *Calandrella* (Red-capped Lark); *Pinarocorys* (Dusky Lark); *Galerida* (Large-billed Lark).

WARBLERS

Flycatchers
Family: Muscicapidae
Genera: *Bradornis* (Marico, Pale and Chat flycatchers); *Muscicapa* (Spotted and African Dusky flycatchers).

Scrub-robins
Family: Muscicapidae
Genus: *Cercotrichas* (Brown, Karoo, Kalahari and White-browed scrub-robins).

Chats & wheatears
Family: Muscicapidae
Genera: *Oenanthe* (Capped, Northern, Pied and Isabelline wheatears and Buff-streaked Chat); *Cercomela* (Karoo, Tractrac, Sickle-winged and Familiar chats); *Saxicola* (African Stonechat and Whinchat).

Weavers
Family: Ploceidae
Genera: *Ploceus* (Chestnut, Village, Southern Brown-throated and Cape weavers, and Lesser and Southern masked-weavers); *Anaplectes* (Red-headed Weaver).

Bishops & allied species
Family: Ploceidae
Genera: *Quelea* (Red-billed, Red-headed and Cardinal queleas); *Euplectes* (Yellow-crowned, Southern Red, Black-winged and Yellow bishops, and White-winged, Red-collared, Fan-tailed, Long-tailed and Yellow-mantled widowbirds).
Family: Viduidae
Genera: *Vidua* (Pin-tailed and Shaft-tailed whydahs, Long-tailed and Broad-tailed paradise-whydahs, and Dusky, Purple, Twinspot and Village indigobirds); *Anomalospiza* (Cuckoo Finch).

Sparrows
Family: Passeridae
Genera: *Passer* (House, Great and Cape sparrows, and Southern and Northern grey-headed sparrows); *Petronia* (Yellow-throated Petronia).

Pipits & longclaws
Family: Motacillidae
Genera: *Anthus* (African, Mountain, Kimberley, Long-billed, Wood, Yellow-breasted, Plain-backed, Buffy, Long-tailed, African Rock, Short-tailed, Bushveld, Striped, Tree and Red-throated pipits); *Macronyx* (Cape Longclaw); *Tmetothylacus* (Golden Pipit).

Canaries & allied species
Family: Fringillidae
Genera: *Crithagra* (Black-throated, Lemon-breasted, Yellow and White-throated canaries, Protea, Black-eared and Streaky-headed seedeaters, and Cape and Drakensberg siskins); *Serinus* (Black-headed Canary); *Emberiza* (Lark-like Bunting).

illustrated glossary

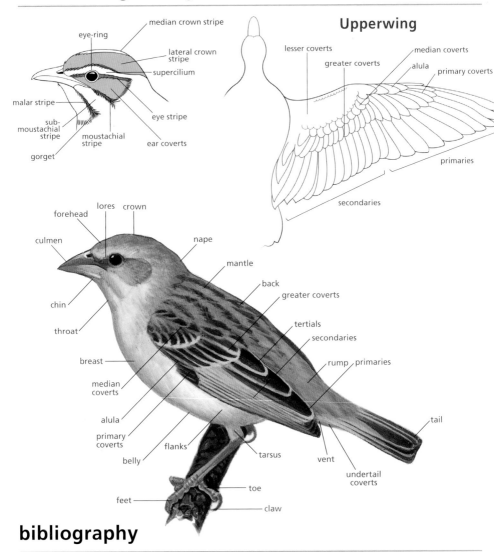

median crown stripe

eye-ring

lateral crown stripe

supercilium

malar stripe

sub-moustachial stripe

moustachial stripe

ear coverts

eye stripe

gorget

Upperwing

lesser coverts

median coverts

greater coverts

alula

primary coverts

primaries

secondaries

lores crown

forehead

culmen

nape

mantle

chin

back

greater coverts

throat

tertials

secondaries

breast

rump primaries

median coverts

alula

tail

primary coverts

flanks

belly

tarsus

vent

toe

feet

undertail coverts

claw

bibliography

Hockey, P, Dean, W & Ryan, P (eds). 2005. *Roberts' Birds of Southern Africa*. John Voelcker Bird Book Fund, Cape Town

Newman, K (revised by Newman, V). 2010. *Newman's Birds of Southern Africa, Commemorative edition* Struik Nature, Cape Town

Sinclair, I, Hockey, P & Tarboton, W. 2002. *Sasol Birds of Southern Africa*, 3rd ed. Struik Nature, Cape Town

Sinclair, I & Ryan, P. 2009. *Complete Photographic Field Guide – Birds of Southern Africa*. Struik Nature, Cape Town

www.indigobirds.com

www.Xeno-canto.org

www.Macauleylibrary.com

Liversidge, R. 'The African Pipit enigma' *Bulletin of the African Bird Club*, volume 5.2, September 1998

index

Acrocephalus
  arundinaceus 31
  baeticatus 30
  gracilirostris 27
  griseldis 27
  palustris 31
  rufescens 29
  schoenobaenus 24
  scirpaceus 30
Ammomanopsis grayi 58
Anaplectes melanotis 94
Anomalospiza imberbis 102
Anthus brachyurus 121
  caffer 121
  cervinus 123
  chloris 118
  cinnamomeus 116
  crenatus 120
  hoeschi 116
  leucophrys 119
  lineiventris 122
  longicaudatus 120
  nyassae 115
  pseudosimilis 117
  similis 117
  trivialis 122
  vaalensis 119
Bishop, Black-winged 104
  Southern Red 104
  Yellow 108
  Yellow-crowned 105
Blouvinkie, Gewone 100
  Groen- 101
  Staal- 101
  Witpoot- 100
Bontrokkie, Europese 90
  Gewone 90
Bradornis infuscatus 76
  mariquensis 77
  pallidus 77
Bradypterus baboecala 32
  barratti 32
  sylvaticus 32
Bunting, Lark-like 130
Calandrella cinerea 69
Calendulauda
  africanoides 68
  albescens 66
  barlowi 66
  burra 67
  erythrochlamys 67
  sabota 72
Canary, Black-headed 130
  Black-throated 126
  Lemon-breasted 126
  White-throated 127
  Yellow 127
Cercomela familiaris 88
  schlegelii excl. subsp.
    namaquensis 89
  schlegelii namaquensis 87

  sinuata 88
  tractrac 87
Cercotrichas coryphoeus 80
  leucophrys 81
  paena 81
  signata 80
Certhilauda
  benguelensis 63
  brevirostris 62
  chuana 64
  curvirostris 62
  semitorquata 64
  subcoronata 63
Chat, Buff-streaked 89
  Familiar 88
  Karoo 87, 89
  Sickle-winged 88
  Tractrac 87
Chersomanes
  albofasciata 65
Cisticola aberrans 41
  aridulus 36
  ayresii 37
  brachypterus 39
  cantans 40
  chiniana 49
  cinnamomeus 38
  erythrops 41
  fulvicapilla 39
  galactotes 42, 46
  juncidis 36
  lais 49
  luapula 43, 46
  natalensis 38, 45
  pipiens 42
  rufilatus 44
  subruficapilla 44, 48
  textrix 37
  tinniens 43, 47
Cisticola, Chirping 42
  Cloud 37
  Croaking 38, 45
  Desert 36
  Grey-backed 44, 48
  Lazy 41
  Levaillant's 43, 47
  Luapula 43, 46
  Pale-crowned 38
  Rattling 49
  Red-faced 41
  Rufous-winged 42, 46
  Short-winged 39
  Singing 40
  Tinkling 44
  Wailing 49
  Wing-snapping 37
  Zitting 36
Crithagra albogularis 127
  atrogularis 126
  citrinipectus 126
  flaviventris 127

  gularis 128
  leucoptera 129
  mennelli 128
  symonsi 131
  totta 131
Emberiza impetuani 130
Eremopterix australis 57
  leucotis 60
  verticalis 60
Euplectes afer 105
  albonotatus 106
  ardens 106
  axillaris 107
  capensis 108
  hordeaceus 104
  macroura 108
  orix 104
  progne 107
Finch, Cuckoo 102
Flap, Geelrug- 108
  Kaapse 108
  Kortstert- 107
  Langstert- 107
  Rooikeel- 106
  Witvlerk- 106
Flycatcher,
  African Dusky 78
  Chat 76
  Marico 77
  Pale 77
  Spotted 78
Galerida magnirostris 73
Heliolais erythropterus 40
Heteromirafra ruddi 59
Heuningvoël, Dunbek- 21
  Skerpbek- 19
  Gevlekte 20
  Groot- 19
  Klein- 20
  Oostelike 21
Hippolais icterina 29
  olivetorum 28
Honeybird, Brown-
    backed 19
  Green-backed 21
Honeyguide, Greater 19
  Lesser 20
  Pallid 21
  Scaly-throated 20
Indicator indicator 19
  meliphilus 21
  minor 20
  variegatus 20
Indigobird, Dusky 100
  Purple 100
  Twinspot 101
  Village 101
Kalkoentjie, Oranjekeel-
    115
Kanarie, Berg- 126
  Bergpietjie- 131

  Geel- 127
  Geelbors- 126
  Kaapse Pietjie- 131
  Streepkop- 128
  Swartkop- 130
  Swartoor- 128
  Witkeel- 127
  Witvlerk- 129
Klappertjie, Hoëveld- 70
  Kaapse 70
  Laeveld- 71
Klipwagter, Berg- 89
Klopkloppie, Bleekkop- 38
  Gevlekte 37
  Kleinste 37
  Landery- 36
  Woestyn- 36
Koester, Berg- 116
  Boom- 122
  Bos- 115
  Bosveld- 121
  Donker- 119
  Geelbors- 118
  Gestreepte 122
  Gewone 116
  Goud- 118
  Kimberley- 117
  Klip- 120
  Kortstert- 121
  Langstert- 120
  Nicholsonse 117
  Rooikeel- 123
  Vaal- 119
Kwelea, Kardinaal- 103
  Rooibek- 102
  Rooikop- 103
Langstertjie, Bruinsy- 51
  Drakensberg- 53
  Karoo- 53
  Namakwa- 54
  Swartband- 51
  Woud- 52
Lark, Agulhas Long-billed 62
  Barlow's 66
  Benguela Long-billed 63
  Botha's 59
  Cape Clapper 70
  Cape Long-billed 62
  Dune 67
  Dusky 69
  Eastern Clapper 70
  Eastern Long-billed 64
  Fawn-coloured 68
  Flappet 71
  Gray's 58
  Karoo Long-billed 63
  Karoo 66
  Large-billed 73
  Melodious 72
  Monotonous 68
  Pink-billed 61

Red 67
Red-capped 69
Rudd's 59
Rufous-naped 74
Sabota 72
Sclater's 73
Short-clawed 64
Spike-heeled 65
Stark's 58
Lewerik, Barlowse 66
Bosveld- 68
Dikbek- 73
Donker- 69
Drakensberg- 59
Duin- 67
Grasveldlangbek- 64
Grysrug- 60
Kaokolangbek- 63
Karoo- 66
Karoolangbek- 63
Kortklou- 64
Namakwa- 73
Namib- 58
Overberglangbek- 62
Pienkbek- 61
Rooi- 67
Rooikop- 69
Rooinek- 74
Rooirug- 60
Sabota- 72
Spot- 72
Swartoor- 57
Vaalbruin- 68
Vaalrivier- 59
Vlakte- 65
Weskuslangbek- 62
Woestyn- 58
Locustella fluviatilis 26
Longclaw, Cape 115
Luscinia luscinia 24
Macronyx capensis 115
Masked-Weaver, Lesser 92
Southern 92
Mirafra africana 74
apiata 70
cheniana 72
fasciolata 70
passerina 68
rufocinnamomea 71
Mossie, Geelvlek- 111
Gewone 111
Groot- 110
Gryskop- 112
Huis- 110
Witkeel- 112
Muscicapa adusta 78
striata 78
Nagtegaal, Lyster- 24
Neddicky 39
Neddikkie 39
Nightingale, Thrush 24
Oenanthe bifasciata 89
isabellina 86
oenanthe 86
pileata 85
pleschanka 84

Oreophilais robertsi 52
Paradise-Whydah,
Broad-tailed 99
Long-tailed 99
Passer diffusus 112
domesticus 110
griseus 112
melanurus 111
motitensis 110
Petronia superciliaris 111
Petronia,
Yellow-throated 111
Phragmacia substriata 54
Phylloscopus trochilus 32
Pinarocorys nigricans 69
Pipit, African Rock 120
African 116
Buffy 119
Bushveld 121
Golden 118
Kimberley 117
Long-billed 117
Long-tailed 120
Mountain 116
Plain-backed 119
Red-throated 123
Short-tailed 121
Striped 122
Tree 122
Wood 115
Yellow-breasted 118
Ploceus capensis 93
cucullatus 93
intermedius 92
rubiginosus 95
velatus 92
xanthopterus 94
Prinia flavicans 51
hypoxantha 53
maculosa 53
subflava 51
Prinia, Black-chested 51
Drakensberg 53
Karoo 53
Tawny-flanked 51
Prodotiscus regulus 19
zambesiae 21
Quelea cardinalis 103
erythrops 103
quelea 102
Quelea, Cardinal 103
Red-billed 102
Red-headed 103
Reed-Warbler, African 30
Basra 27
Eurasian 30
Great 31
Rooibekkie, Koning- 98
Pylstert- 98
Rush-Warbler, Little 32
Sanger, Basrariet- 27
Breëstert- 26
Europese Riet- 31
Europese Vlei- 24
Grootriet- 31
Hermanse Riet- 30

Hof- 32
Kaapse Riet- 27
Kaapse Vlei- 32
Kleinriet- 30
Knysnaruigte- 32
Olyfboom- 28
Rooibruinriet- 29
Rooivlerk- 40
Ruigte- 32
Spot- 29
Sprinkaan- 26
Tuin- 28
Witkeel- 25
Saxicola rubetra 90
rubetra 90
torquatus 90
Schoenicola brevirostris 26
Scrub-Robin, Brown 80
Kalahari 81
Karoo 80
White-browed 81
Seedeater, Black-eared 128
Protea 129
Streaky-headed 128
Serinus alario 130
Siskin, Cape 131
Drakensberg 131
Skaapwagter, Bont- 84
Europese 86
Hoëveld- 85
Isabella- 86
Slangverklikker 80
Sparrow, Cape 111
Great 110
House 110
Southern
Grey-headed 112
Northern
Grey-headed 112
Sparrowlark, Black-eared 57
Chestnut-backed 60
Grey-backed 60
Spekvreter, Gewone 88
Karoo- 87
Karoo- 89
Vlakte- 88
Woestyn- 87
Spizocorys conirostris 61
fringillaris 59
sclateri 73
starki 58
Stonechat, African 90
Streepkop, Vaal- 130
Swamp-Warbler, Greater 29
Lesser 27
Sylvia borin 28
communis 25
Tinktinkie, Bosveld- 49
Groot- 38, 45
Grysrug- 44, 48
Huil- 49
Kortvlerk- 39
Luapula- 43, 46
Lui- 41
Piepende 42
Rooi- 44

Rooiwang- 41
Singende 40
Swartrug- 42, 46
Vlei- 43, 47
Tmetothylacus tenellus 118
Vidua chalybeata 101
codringtoni 101
funerea 100
macroura 98
obtusa 99
paradisaea 99
purpurascens 100
regia 98
Vink, Breëstertparadys- 99
Gewone Paradys- 99
Goudgeel- 105
Kleingeel- 92
Koekoek- 102
Rooi- 104
Swartkeelgeel- 92
Vuurkop- 104
Vlieëvanger Europese 78
Donker- 78
Groot- 76
Marico- 77
Muiskleur- 77
Warbler, Barratt's 32
Broa   led 26
C
Na
Olive-tree 28
Red-winged 40
River 26
Roberts's 52
Sedge 24
Willow 32
Weaver, Cape 93
Chestnut 95
Red-headed 94
Southern Brown-
throated 94
Village 93
Wewer, Bontrug- 93
Bruin- 95
Bruinkeel- 94
Kaapse 93
Rooikop- 94
Wheatear, Capped 85
Isabelline 86
Northern 86
Pied 84
Whinchat 90
Whitethroat, Common 25
Whydah, Pin-tailed 98
Shaft-tailed 98
Widowbird, Fan-tailed 107
Long-tailed 107
Red-collared 106
White-winged 106
Yellow-mantled 108
Wipstert, Bruin- 80
Gestreepte 81
Kalahari- 81